T0018322

What We Don't Know

Ruminations on the professional and life experiences of a washed ashore ex-sea captain, notorious pirate bar owner, philanthropist and keen observer of human behavior, and how these observation and thoughts point directly to the certain existence of God.

CAPTAIN ERIC F. SCHILLER

Cover Photo by Ray Turkin

WHAT WE DON'T KNOW

iUniverse books may be ordered through booksellers or by contacting:

iUniverse
1663 Liberty Drive
Bloomington, IN 47403
www.iuniverse.com
1-800-Authors (1-800-288-4677)

ISBN: 978-1-5320-8732-5 (sc)
ISBN: 978-1-5320-8734-9 (hc)
ISBN: 978-1-5320-8733-2 (e)

Library of Congress Control Number: 2019917861

Print information available on the last page.

iUniverse rev. date: 01/11/2020

Q: What is the difference between a sea story and a fairy tale?

A: A fairy tale begins with “Once upon a time …”

A sea story begins with “This is no shit.”

To John McPhee, author of *Oranges* and *Looking for a Ship*,
without whom I would not have been inspired to even try

Introduction

Chaim Moishe Moskowitz was the most engaging, magnetic, and effective professor I ever studied with in a sixteen-year academic career. He was installed in the Department of Marine Engineering at the United States Merchant Marine Academy in Great Neck, New York, in the 1960s and 1970s.

A pugnacious man, he was earnest, honest, and straightforward as hell itself. He looked like a lightweight fighter and carried himself like he could and would handle himself easily and effectively. He had spent many years at sea in the engine rooms of merchant vessels circling the globe on all of the world's oceans and seas. Each one of those assignments added to his encyclopedic knowledge of the world.

He was not a young man when he was lecturing midshipmen on the art and science of marine engineering in the early 1970s. He possessed a humor based on thought and irony. I recognized him as a thoughtful person who had the rare ability to listen as well as lecture. That was surprising considering our section of twenty-year-old know-it-all midshipmen had little to say that was meaningful in any way. I don't know how he stayed awake and interested when any of us were bloviating.

His style of teaching was simple: he would pace back in forth in front of our class and ask leading questions of his charges. He would purse his lips to our answers and furrow his brow in consideration and sometimes consternation, to be accurate. He might actually tug at his chin for affect. If your answer hit the nail on the head, he would turn to face you and point at you while nodding his head. High praise it was.

He always wore a white, starched lab coat over a khaki uniform with khaki tie and highly polished black shoes. He sported small gold eagle insignia on his shirt collars, as senior faculty at military schools often do. He had a remarkably full head of salt-and-pepper hair for a man his age. It was parted on the right and glossy from some type of pomade or other goose grease.

I have always believed that he learned his method of questioning students from whomever he had studied Talmud with in New York, where he grew up a Jew. I do not know this for a fact because, although we spoke quite often, I never felt I had license to ask him personal questions. Certainly I realized that coming up the ranks in the merchant marine in the postwar years and through the 1950s was not easy for a fellow carrying the name of Chaim Moishe Moskowitz. Maybe that was where the deep notch in the bridge of his nose came from.

It was a wonderful class. I never enjoyed another more or learned more useful things from one. We talked about engineering and machinery about 20 percent of the time. The rest of the time, we discussed and examined seagoing life and the philosophy of many things of widely disparate subjects, from politics to honor, careers, family life, and the thinking behind the philosophy of machine design, which turns out in most cases to solve most problems in our field. If you can gain a working understanding about what the design engineers were trying to accomplish, you'll find yourself holding the keys to many of those answers.

One time toward the beginning of the semester, he passed out a duplicated document to the class that Henry Kissinger, then US secretary of state and well-known ladies' man, believe it or not, had written. He asked us to read it and be prepared to discuss it at the next day's class. Clearly Kissinger could be worth reading, but no one had any illusions that Kissinger had made any notable contributions to the field of marine engineering. We never heard of a Kissinger turbine or a Kissinger valve.

Of course, anybody who has read anything by the esteemed Dr. Kissinger will know with certainty that there is no tougher slogging than a read through anything Kissinger. None of us could make heads or tails out of what Kissinger was trying to say. It could have been written in a foreign language for our purposes. We came to class the next day bewildered and chagrined … to a man, each and every one of us. There were bright people in that bunch, but nobody could get anywhere with the assignment.

Professor M. called on the first midshipman and asked what he had learned from the assignment. Red-faced and dispirited, our classmate had to admit that he didn't understand a single sentence. The rest of us agreed, nodding heads and murmuring in support.

Professor M. broke in. "Well, there you have it, gentlemen." His arms were held out wide. "You fellows have chosen a practical and pragmatic field, not academics, politics, or governmental service. Lives depend on clarity and brevity, and success or failure hang on those same things. So if any of you ever turn in a paper to me that reads like last night's assignment, I will fail you."

He waved his arms. "If a man can't express his ideas, any or all of them, fully in simple and plain language in one or two pages, then he, gentlemen, is a bullshit artist. I cast no aspersions toward the undisputedly brilliant Dr. Kissinger, but there's a time and a place for such theatrics. This isn't it. Further, I won't be lecturing to any bullshit artists around here. You remember that!"

He uttered *bullshit* with a puff of his lips on the exhaled *b* as punctuation to further drive home his point. He was obviously performing and having fun while doing it.

Well, I have always remembered the point of that lesson. In the writing of this book and in the effort of making the point I'll attempt to make, I came up short in sheer volume of material. The simple fact is that I'm not attempting rocket surgery here by any means. It's simply the presentation of an idea or two about the realization of how things are or seem to be and the probability of what probability probably is. Along with that and considering the realization that compared to the rest of the cosmos, humankind is, on the face of things, not much more consequential than intergalactic flea dirt.

Rather than dilute the essence of the idea, spoiling what I had already written and risking the posthumous wrath of Professor Chaim Moishe Moskowitz, captain, United States Merchant Service (deceased), I took the only sensible option available. I stopped writing. Done. Cold turkey. Quit.

I was left with perhaps a lengthy article but not a book. I left the manuscript alone for quite some time to pursue other interests like paying the mortgage, putting food on the table for the children, traveling with the lovely Mrs. S., bringing up three kids in an upside-down and certifiably insane world, and keeping the business in business—you know, the same things that all the other really fortunate people get to do in life, if lucky.

Early last year and forty-plus years removed from Professor Moskowitz's near-magical classroom on the third floor of Fureseth Hall, I was down at the bar the fetching Mrs. S. and I now operate. I was talking to some foreign merchant seamen who were signed on a large bulker then docked at the port of Tampa, only a stone's throw away, loading bulk phosphate and bound for God only knows where. It's just one of the many seagoing vessels that call here in my adopted hometown of Tampa. Very nice people, humble, polite, and earnest; they never change. They're just working people trying to earn an honest living the hard way and trying to get home in one piece before the wife and kids forget who they are entirely.

We were having a fine time, debating the merits of the latest rye whiskey phenomena, tasting those against some local and various small-batch bourbons, and regaling each other with sea stories about things that happen to sailors and ships in weather rough or clear, at sea or ashore. I may have taken the opportunity to introduce these fellows to what is locally considered the world's best Manhattan, lovingly and carefully prepared by yours truly. I digress. I apologize.

It's always a privilege to share some time with these men and women and with some nice hand-rolled cigars, Churchills preferably, Dominican long-leaf filler, Connecticut-shade wrappers made by my neighbors, descendants of master Cuban cigar rollers and lifelong Ybor City residents.

Truth be told, I have a very soft spot in my heart for all these sailors, having spent more than twenty-five years at sea myself and possessing some understanding of the game. Thus, our bartenders will testify that not a lot of money is changing hands when Captain Schiller is entertaining merchant seaman at the bar.

There, only a fathom or so south of the north bar rail, it occurred to me that those sea stories, each one true and every one a left-handed twist from the workaday reality in the normal universe of regular people who do not go to sea for a living, there might be something of interest to a reader or two. I decided to weave sea stories in among the chapters of a book concerning philosophy and psychology, tempered with theology and probability of sorts.

In actuality, two books are melded here as one. Whether or not that will work out and will be enjoyable, entertaining, or successful should and will be judged solely by you, the reader. I'm hoping this is a productive endeavor. Regardless, it certainly has been tremendous fun and a great joy in my life. Enjoy!

Captain Eric Schiller
The Wheelhouse at Gaspar's Grotto
Tampa, Florida
2018

CHAPTER 1

Hong Kong, 1973

I was a teenage deck cadet aboard the SS *American Liberty* when we tied up to a North Point pier very near downtown Hong Kong one sultry Southest Asia summer morning, just after dawn. I clearly remember it was August 1973. The harbor was so smooth that morning I actually recall writing "greasy" as the sea state in the morning's weather report. That was more a function of the dead-calm weather than a commentary on the water quality. The star ferry was not too far away, making its approach to the Kowloon ferry terminal, packed with commuters, businesspeople, workers, and visitors. Victoria Peak jutted skyward just astern of us as the light improved after sunrise. Two seagulls flapped, pecked, and squawked at each other, fighting over some type of floating carrion. It was another bustling day beginning in the crossroads of Southeast Asia.

We prepared to discharge our containers in a time before dedicated container cranes had been built anywhere in Hong Kong. A six-hour stevedoring job today took more than three days back then, and that was quite all right with me. Three-plus days in Hong Kong held possibilities for a nineteen-year-old. Hong Kong was a very different place in those days from what it is now. There were considerably more one and two-story masonry buildings, sheet metal sheds, and lean-to-like shanties than the steel-and-glass skyscrapers that grow out of the island's rocky formations now. There were far fewer business suits and more Asian laborer's garb: conical-shaped straw coolie hats, pajamas, and bare feet. There were more actual neighborhoods, street markets, and gin mills named Florida Bar and New York Bar, having nothing at all to do with Florida or New York than there were to be in the very near future. There were working men, working women, and more than a fair share of working girls.

The ubiquitous "bum" boats were coming alongside with barefoot locals climbing up bamboo ladders fastened with hemp rope to set up shop and sell the sailors trinkets they needed and things they couldn't possibly use but would buy anyway. Many street artists among the bum boats were offering to paint portraits or pictures of the sailor's loved ones from any dog-eared photo the client could provide. They did astoundingly competent work. Cooking fires were lit on our steel deck with boiling pots of ginseng-spiced dishes being prepared under the stowed lifeboats and consumed by squatting men and women, some well into their eighties by the look of them.

Working and living among them, for only a short time, is how most sailors I know have become socially liberal people without even trying to understand or accept that label. You will learn a lot simply by opening your eyes, ears, and heart. It's something you learn by living, not by sitting in a classroom at an Ivy League or junior college, listening to a professional graduate student pontificate on nonsense with a straight face due to their selflessly unaware ignorance.

Seagoing just may be the world's finest, most intensely rigorous education, however informal, unstructured, or lightly documented. And it may be the unintended definition of continuing education because as long as someone is sailing, they are learning through new experiences. And what's the best part? They pay you to do it! What could be better?

Outside the barbed wire gate of the sparsely paved, multiacre yard that passed for a container facility was a ramshackle neighborhood of low buildings of indeterminate age and absolutely no architectural merit. It was made up of many small storefronts and shops to service the people who lived among the hodgepodge of industry, manufacturing, residential, retail, and public buildings. I don't think there were any zoning regulations in Hong Kong in 1973. But it worked and did so beautifully. The streets were narrow, and the trucks that pulled the containers to and from the yard roared loudly as they continuously belched oily, black smoke into the air, only inches from the sidewalk, day and night.

Within a stone's throw of the gate was a small shop we called the *podunk*, a word, I'm nearly certain, that was appropriated from the GIs who were attempting to survive the bloody jungle fighting not all that far away in Vietnam, simultaneously occurring while we were tied up there in Hong Kong. The podunk sold some foodstuff, soft drinks, some toiletries, a few newspapers, charcoal, various cigarettes, and other useful things that the neighborhood folk and sailors needed. If they had sold flies, they could have retired. They had an impressive stock.

Most importantly to us, the podunk sold ice-cold beer. Every day at coffee time, exactly 10:00 a.m. and 3:00 p.m., per the union contract, we would leave the vessel, scurry over to the podunk, and down a cold beer or two. I wish I could remember the brand. It could have been Tiger or Tsing Tao, but I can't be sure, and it really doesn't matter. We would sit on two ragtag repurposed automotive bench seats on the sidewalk, right in front of the shop.

To the right was a grammar school. A bell would ring, and the small kids, boys and girls, would pour out onto the sidewalk for recess. Several concurrent games of tag would break out on the sidewalk among the youngsters. We had the best seats in the house. Many of the children would flirt, smile, and giggle with the seamen, enjoying their temporary freedom in those still mornings. The joyous noise those gorgeous children in white shirts and blue-and-green plaid uniforms produced would often bring tears to some of our lonely shipmates who were so far, in distance and time, from their own families. Seagoing is often a lonely affair; you can trust me on that.

Then the school bell would ring. The teachers would chase the running children back inside, and we would finish our beers and go back to work on our waiting ship. Among the most indelible and beautiful memories of my life were those children.

On one of those mornings, we were sitting there as the children were being shepherded back inside their school. We were finishing up our beers when down the street came a man, dressed like a farmer but also wearing shoes, leading an ox by a rope connected to a ring in the ox's nose. He stopped outside the butcher shop, just on the far side of the school. The shop was open to the sidewalk and was entirely tiled with white porcelain tiles. It had glass display cases and more flies than you could imagine. It was quiet on the street. Not long after 10:00 a.m., out from the butcher shop came the butcher, carrying a sledgehammer.

We all slowly stood. No one talked, transfixed. The children were not outside at that moment. With a single long, looping, circular swing, backward and then forward with a grunt, the butcher hit the ox on the top of his head. Down went the ox, without a sound. There was no pain, nothing. I distinctly remember feeling a touch unsteady and queasy.

"Holy cow!" someone said ironically.

I put down my unfinished beer. Several of the other guys did the same. We turned and filed quietly back aboard the vessel, single file, a few minutes before we normally would have.

That same day, after an afternoon's work onboard the ship, at the afternoon coffee time, some of us decided it was time to go back to the podunk and have—what else—a cold beer. We stood on the sidewalk outside of the podunk, looking up the street. The butcher was standing on the sidewalk, squirting water out of a black rubber hose, old and leaking in several places. He was washing the remnants of his morning's work off the sidewalk and into the storm drain, from where it shortly and ultimately found its way into Hong Kong Harbor to feed the fish.

The display cases in his shop were full. Strings of ox parts were hanging from hooks in the shop. Flies were still buzzing around. The children were chasing around and about. Delightful squeals were carried through the street, drowned out only by the periodic roar of a truck pulling another rust-stained container away from the yard.

I don't think it's much like that in Hong Kong anymore.

My late father, a talented engineer and a far better man than most I've met, when faced with a big task, often would ask us, "How do you eat an elephant?"

He'd immediately reply, "One bite at a time."

So where do we take the first bite? The answer is probably with people. In an attempt to propose and advance a theory concerning philosophy, theology, and humor, it would seem that is a logical jumping in place.

It's a fascinating phenomenon, consciousness and thought in the biological organism known as the human. It's something we take for granted but is certainly no simple or trivial matter. Why? From a human being's perspective, the only one available to us in this examination, there is no more complicated organism on the planet. That is neither good nor bad. It's simply a fact. Or is it? It seems to be a fact from everything we know.

But from what we do not know, there might be another set of facts or perhaps even another perspective. Both or either amount to the same thing, an altered perception of reality or what we would normally think of as reality. Biologically, humans are a species that is really no more complicated than a great number of others that we share the planet with. What sets us apart is the brain we possess and some limited physical attributes that allow us to use the abilities of that brain.

The thumb and the hand—plus the brain—equals a superior ability for us to develop and use tools in furtherance of the goals the brain and our wills choose for us. We are natural builders. We have the ability to accomplish work. Just look at the surface of the planet, for better or for worse, it can be argued. And we have the will and the other mental tools and abilities to make that happen.

Our existence is a given for us in modern society. We are all tasked to find something to do with all our tools. People become specialized based on their talents and abilities—physical, mental, and emotional—and those things that many consider gifts. Gifts from whom? From driving a train to raising a family, drawing pictures, stopping crime, and committing crime, each of us is able to have a role in what becomes a society. We each are not only allowed but required to find our place in the order of such social things. The rest of the animals do not do that to nearly such a large extent.

Our keen eyes allow us to see in all conditions to protect ourselves and order our world the way we see it. The body allows us, with the brain, to stand erect to move in every direction to get ourselves out of, or oftentimes into, trouble.

The memory, keen in a human, allows us to learn and retrieve thoughts and build our experiences that can define and even give purpose to our lives. We can accomplish more work and coexist with others.

Humans have been roaming the earth in one form or another for hundreds of thousands of years, or so the scientists tell us. There is no reason to doubt them. Or is there? Recently in the scope of such things, as time goes, Charles Darwin postulated that there have been evolutionary changes to human beings to such a degree that we might not recognize our predecessors, stating that we have descended from apes, our prehensile tail bones are proof, and crawled out of a pool of slime in the beginning to walk erect. Are we obliged to accept Darwin's beliefs? This is one of a universe of things we don't know.

It is understood in certain quarters that all the things humans know, the facts, and the unknown are accumulating at a hyperbolic rate. In fact, it is postulated that 90 percent of humankind's knowledge has been learned or perhaps gleaned from the chaff of the rest of the physical world in only the last two hundred years. True or false, this is an astounding assertion.

Think of what we know. Look carefully at the whole of humankind's knowledge. There are many fields, facts, endeavors, avocations, and fields of knowledge that are rapidly being filled out, and if not, they are simply populated. And doubtless the curve that traces the sum of all this knowledge is rapidly escalating. Of that, there can be no argument. New fields, never imagined only a few years ago, are developing rapidly. Who could have imagined gene therapy, computer science, or nuclear energy only a mere 150 years ago? Even science fiction could not have envisioned these things. And even science fiction itself has evolved for that matter! Do we not see the forest for the trees?

Consider this recent saying of nebulous origin: "You don't know what you don't know." Some clever lady or gentleman with time on his or her hands may write a doctoral thesis in sociology or anthropology on the genesis of that saying. Regardless, there is no argument there either. You don't know what you don't know—unless you decide to look carefully at what it actually is that you don't know.

Who hasn't felt as the years tick by quickly in our human life span that the older we get and the more we learn, the less we know? It seems to be true with individuals and, I propose likewise, society in general. Wise people eventually join this club. Please notice the word *wise* is used. It's substantially different from *educated.* And those with overactive egos or slow wits may not get there from here at all. Wisdom is nothing if not elusive—always earned, never bought, and never sold

CHAPTER 2

Somewhere north of 40 degrees North Latitude in the Pacific, 1978

A sea captain, not highly educated in any formal sense but very wise nonetheless, once told the following story to his third mate, the youngest and most junior of officers on a seagoing merchant vessel.

"When I was a twenty-one-year-old third mate," the old man began, "I was sure I knew everything. I didn't mind sharing my vast knowledge with anybody who wanted to hear it—and with some who didn't.

"A few years went by, and I earned the rank of second mate. As my responsibilities for the navigation of the vessel weighed on me, I started to understand the depth and breadth of my position. It was then that I began to doubt exactly how much I really knew.

"After several more years at sea, I successfully passed the exams to become a chief mate. There was so much to know, new requirements, experiences, and responsibilities. Billions of dollars in environmental liability. Hundreds of millions of dollars worth of cargo. The entire deck department's scheduling, safety, productivity, and duties of the junior officers—all under my supervision. It was humbling.

"I spent many years in the chief mate's position, feeling the weight of that job on my shoulders, coming into middle age, and starting a family. It was very sobering stuff. I was finally qualified to sit for the exam for the master's license. I was fortunate enough to pass. More years went by while I waited for a position to open up by death, dismissal, or retirement. When a position did become available, I was lucky enough to be chosen to fill it. I assumed ultimate and final responsibility for everything in our small shipboard world as master of the vessel. I quickly realized that although well prepared, there was so much I did not know and had yet to learn."

The captain stabbed himself in the chest with an arthritic thumb. "But I knew that everything was going to be just fine because I had a third mate who knew everything!" He grinned a Cheshire cat grin at that.

You can probably guess that I was that third mate whom the captain told this story to. What you may not realize is that in the blink of an eye, as time flies, I became that captain, the old man in the story as well.

The wheel continues to turn. It always does. That's what wheels do.

So there we have it, the awareness of what we do not know. This is a fairly obscure (perhaps underserved in today's vernacular) principle in history. It is the flip side of what we do know. It seems to be the mirror image of what we have understanding of. If knowledge is the yin, then the unknown is the yang. For everything known, there is a direct path to more—much more in actuality—that is yet unknown.

If we go back to the premise that the vast majority of humankind's knowledge has been learned in only the last few centuries, one can see that for centuries there wasn't much to know in any and every case. Thus, the indicators of what we did not know were few.

A common proverb in our American South is, "When you are up to your ass in alligators, it's hard to remember that your initial objective was to drain the swamp." And so it was with the civilizations in prehistoric, ancient, and medieval times. Of primary importance was eating and defending the village against any number of lethal occurrences. Keeping the children alive until they could fend for themselves was a task unto itself, and not always successful.

From marauding bands of God-knows-who to forced conscription in any number of organizations from the czar's army (as happened to my grandfather Jacob Kushner) to the slaves who built the wonders of the ancient world, life was primarily and correctly focused on the alligators. There was little time to dream of things yet undiscovered. That's one reason why Aristotle, Plato, and other ancient philosophers have endured. Their thinking was both early and original to civilization, and there were very few working philosophers among the ancients. It was hard to make a living in the field of philosophy back then. But civilizations grew up and around their thoughts. They expanded the universe of thought from their own considerations. Still, it seems, they did not think about what they did not know, with the exception of the heavens, which have always been the source of mind-boggling stimulation and mystery prior to almost any other thought. They picked the low-hanging fruit of what was easiest to know among what was readily evident to them in an effort to make sense of what was before them.

These thinkers applied themselves to real-life situations, problems, and a body of work developed from the thoughts surrounding those ruminations. Others, like Archimedes, who overran a bathtub filling with water, and Isaac Newton, who was hit on the head by a falling apple, were exceptional observers of the physical world. Their investigations unraveled physical laws. Einstein used mathematics to explore new worlds and what he did not know. Perhaps the only absolutely pure discipline on earth, a discipline where truth is undeniable and unchangeable, mathematics delivered him to conclusions that would remain unproven for decades for lack of the physical tools to measure and verify his equations. Einstein spent his days pondering the unknowable and came closer than almost any other humans to know what he did not know.

The point of this tiptoeing over stepping-stones in the stream of knowledge and barely getting our feet wet is that there has not been, until recently, enough knowledge to demarcate a jumping-off place into the antiknowledge, or the unknown, for use of a better word.

Perhaps we should call this discipline, or field of exploration, *noknowlogy*. Why not? There are far less cogent "ologies" today and many more of them than ever before in fact. Many of them are frivolous, at best. Each is a body of knowledge, a course of study, a major field of study at prestigious universities where pampered young skulls full of feathers oft try to meld the publications of their professor's meaningless yet profitable pabble (pablum + babble) into their own paying careers. So noknowlogy is the entire universe of things that we do not know. It might be what we will never know, for any one of a number of reasons.

Perhaps the knowledge is too much for our puny brains to handle. Consider this: as wonderful as dogs are, learning spherical trigonometry is not going to happen for a canine. There are just simply not enough neurons in that gloriously fuzzy skull. There is not enough "there" there, to continue the overuse of that recently popularized and badly overused colloquial platitude. Perhaps the entire human race will be extinct from our mismanagement of our affairs, from a marauding meteor, a biological happenstance that causes a mass see-you-later-Charlie, a runaway artificial intelligence, or something intelligent (or not) from deep space.

Maybe it's something as straightforward as a gaseous cloud from the tail of a streaking comet. Maybe the sun will unexpectedly explode. Nine minutes later, we are all ancient history.

Maybe there has to be more groundwork before we know what we don't know. Certainly you can't build the next floor in a skyscraper without building the one before it. Perhaps it's just simply not time for us to know what we do not know. Chew on that a bit while the following sea story entertains you. Remember, this is no shit!

CHAPTER 3

The Hawaiian Archepelago to Singapore 1990

In the summer of 1990, we sailed from Honolulu, Hawaii, for Singapore's Jurong Shipyard. We were on an old single-boiler steam tanker built in Newport News with lots of miles and lots of problems. Rumor had it that the steel plates she was built from were recycled WWII tanks. She was a tough old bird. There might have been truth in that rumor. The main condenser was leaking badly. Saltwater was entering the steam cycle (which is very bad), and we were continuously injecting the condenser with sawdust, bag after bag. In effect, the sawdust would work its way into the leaks and then expand in the leak to seal it, an eighteenth-century fix to a twentieth-century problem. The evaporators couldn't make fresh water as fast as we were using it because the boiler was on continuous blow in order to keep the salinity down in the boiler's feedwater.

So we steamed across the Pacific Ocean, looking for and chasing down rain clouds. We would get in a rainstorm and try to stay there as long as we could. The rainwater that fell on the three-acre deck was channeled into spill tanks normally used to contain accidental oil spills. When the tanks were full, we would pump the rainwater down to the engine room for use as boiler feed water. What a way to run a railroad! Luckily, it rained often on that trip.

Without further problems on an otherwise uneventful Pacific crossing, we took arrival at Horsberg Lighthouse in Singapore late one very hazy afternoon. And just in time, the water tanks were nearly empty! I don't think my chief engineer was ever happier to arrive at a shipyard.

There's always plenty to do in these shipyards. It's more work than you have hands or time for. We shut down all the auxiliaries in preparation for a major overhaul that was to take several months. This left us with no air-conditioning or potable water and a totally uninhabitable vessel.

With the help of the ship's local agent, I made arrangements to get hotel rooms for the whole contingent. Some would be flying home; others would stay the entire yard period and steam the vessel back across the Pacific eastbound when the work was completed. I spent a lot of time acting as a travel agent. We negotiated a fair deal for a block of rooms for two months from the Mandarin Oriental Hotel on Orchard Road.

We were right in the heart of Singapore. We had to make one slight accommodation to the hotel. Since we were coming to the hotel from work every day directly from the shipyard, we were typically a very dirty lot. The hotel did not want us using the front entrance with all the dignitaries, tourists, and business travelers who used the hotel. So our bunch went in and out from a loading dock around the side entrance and took the service elevators up to our rooms, where we would clean up and then be free to use the regular elevators. It was easy enough.

I had told the crew before we arrived that I expected them to work hard and to play hard. That was *de rigueur*. I made sure they knew they were in one of the world's best ports, the per diem was generous, and I would deal with it if they couldn't make the best of it. I made it a point to tell them that if there were any problems, they would be on a plane headed stateside in short order.

Early on we had one fellow, one of the engine gang, not acclimating to it after a few days of the early-morning routine, bus ride, soup for breakfast, shipyard work, bus ride back, evenings out, and hotel. He made it a point to rain on everybody else's parade, whining and complaining. The food, heat, and schedule, none was to his liking.

One morning while we were waiting for the morning bus to the shipyard, I went over to him and handed him an airplane ticket. "I know you're having a miserable time here, staying in this luxury hotel, eating some of the world's best food on the company's nickel, and consorting with some of the most exotic women on the planet, so I want you to go back upstairs, pack your bags, and be back down here at nine a.m. sharp. The agent has a ride arranged for you to the airport. Good luck."

He went slack-jawed and then started to argue, but I said nothing and pointed to the elevator. You could have heard a pin drop. There was not a single complaint about anything from anyone for the next two months in Singapore. Evidently life had gotten very good.

In those years, the Mandarin Oriental Hotel was as nice a hotel as Singapore had to offer, and along with the guest rooms, there were floors upon floors of function and banquet rooms. They were beautifully appointed, and the food was fabulous there. We would spend hours on the mezzanine over the lobby having an ice-cold beer or three, watching people and observing the groups come and go. The clientele coming in and out of that hotel for functions were always dressed to the nines.

The hotel's cocktail waitresses wore sleek, long black satin dresses with high collars, colorfully embroidered dragon decorations, and a slit on the side that started at the hem and went as high up as your imagination could go. It was special, particularly when they would seamlessly, slowly, and gracefully fall to their knees on the carpet next to your chair in order to take your drink order.

Some of the men I had in the crew were farm boys from Middle America. They couldn't get over that. It was not at all like ordering a tall stack, side of grits, and a cup of coffee, extra cream, at Mabel's Highway 52 Family Diner out on SR52 just past Pleasantville.

Out in front of the hotel, overlooking Orchard Road, was an expansive, elevated *Porte cochere.* The apron was so large that they would park the luxury automobiles on it, directly across from the front doors nearest the street. It was not uncommon to see Rolls-Royces, Bentleys, Ferraris, and any number of large German marques there. That in itself was unusual because in those days Singapore taxed automobiles heavily on the displacement of their engines. Only the very well-to-do could afford to drive a large automobile in Singapore.

The porte cochere was always a beehive of activity of people coming and going as well as cabs, cars, and jitneys. In charge of that whole intricate ballet was the head bellman, a Sikh whom we nicknamed the Sergeant Major. Standing about six and a half feet tall, he was the size of a mature elm tree. As brown as a nut, he had slits for eyes and sported a heavily waxed handlebar moustache that would make any member of a barbershop quartet proud. It was salt and pepper, as were his bushy eyebrows.

Most striking was his posture. He stood bolt upright, ramrod straight. He oozed dignity and serious business. He wore an immaculate white silk uniform with white gloves and a double-breasted jacket adorned with polished brass buttons. His shoes were polished so highly that you could see your reflection in them. Braided gold epaulets were on his shoulders. Most striking was a huge, white silk turban wrapped around his head and reaching skyward another foot. It was punctuated by a large, red ruby cabochon in a gold setting, right in the center, above his forehead. The only effect missing was a sword. The uniform, I suppose, was a leftover remnant of Singapore's colonial past, a subject of much contentious discussion these days, but not then. One thing was certain: this was a fellow not to be trifled with.

He ran the rope lines and queues with military precision, thus the Sergeant Major label. He would blow the whistle he carried on a braided lanyard around his neck, and a cab would speed in, discharge passengers, reload, and be gone faster than a pit stop at the twenty-four hours of Le Mans. Woe be it to the driver who dawdled. No one wanted to be on the bad side of the Sergeant Major.

So one night after a late dinner at the hotel, I decided to jump in a cab and head out to listen to some live music. The porte cochere was very busy and buzzing with activity. The lines formed were full of ladies and gentlemen dressed formally, many of those gentlemen in tuxedos and the women in long gowns. Evidently they were leaving a swanky function. Private cars of all sorts were picking them up, and mixed in were the cabs. The parking apron was full of Singapore's finest luxury automobiles, as always. Drivers were standing alongside, some polishing their charges and some not.

The night was wonderful—balmy, tropical, and clear. It smelled like Singapore, with all due fond reminiscence and respect. As I was moving steadily toward the front of the queue, I remember thinking how lucky I was to have such a swell job that I could experience all this and get paid for it too.

The Sergeant Major gave a short blast of his whistle and motioned a cab from his right to pull up. I noticed a blue-and-white, small, boxy, Japanese four-door with a bad muffler, carpeted dashboard, and a gold-tasseled religious charm hanging from the mirror like every public conveyance in Manila or other major Southeast Asian city carries. It roared up the ramp like an airplane, at similar speed, as the Sergeant Major stepped from the curb and whipped open the rear driver's side door, as the vehicle screeched to a stop to let the passengers out before reloading with another society lady and her escort. The Sergeant Major came to attention, holding the door handle firmly in his right hand, palm up.

As soon as the door opened, I recognized one of my crew members inside the cab. The only problem was that he was tightly tangled up with one of the local women. The two, nearly naked, were very obviously caught *en flagrante delicto*. I recall him looking out the door into the waiting crowd with his great toothy smile. He and I locked eyes momentarily, one of the most uncomfortable moments I can remember ever having. He had his left arm resting on the back of the rear seat, obviously happy and proud of this performance.

I, on the other hand, was speechless. And although far from prudish, after the observance of a lifetime's worth of juvenile and inappropriate stunts, I was appalled. Also speechless were the several dozen society ladies and their husbands and escorts. There was a collective gasp from behind the rope lines. Swooning ensued.

The Sergeant Major, standing rigidly upright at attention and therefore not seeing what was happening inside the car, bent down to see what all the fuss was about. I was near him, and I saw his neck and cheeks turn from nut brown to beet red. I thought his turban was going to rocket off his head skyward and proceed into near-earth orbit. He turned, and with his left hand, he poked the driver through the open window and started to yell at him loudly in a tongue I did not understand. The meaning, however, was perfectly clear. His language approximated staccato machine-gun fire. The driver stepped hard on the gas and burned rubber down the other side of the porte cochere as the Sergeant Major slammed the rear door so hard the car shook.

My crew member twisted his head, looked back at the carnage through the back window, and grinned, admiring the aftermath of his deliberate and very public indiscretion. The gold tassel hanging from the rearview mirror gyrated wildly.

The whole episode lasted only a few seconds. I'm sure anybody who was there that night to witness it will not forget it.

A few minutes went by, and I was in my own cab, heading uptown. I expected to hear from the hotel's management but never did.

The next day, I sought out my misbehaving crew member, and we had a short but pointed discussion. The gist of it was, "Not funny, son! Try hard not to do that again, or you'll be on a plane home *tout de suite*."

The rhythm of life went on in Singapore.

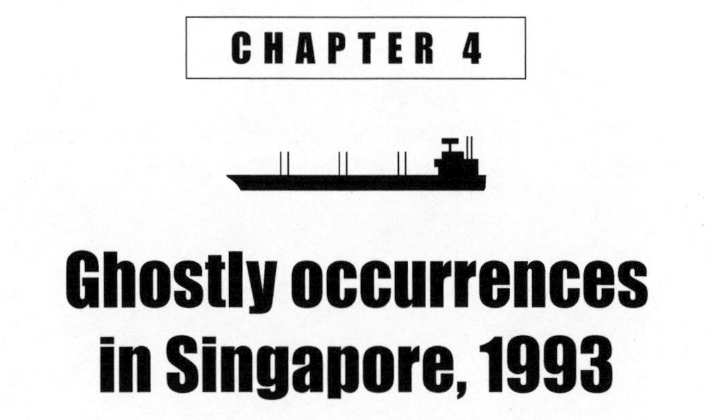

CHAPTER 4

Ghostly occurrences in Singapore, 1993

The occult can be defined as the knowledge of the paranormal as opposed to what we recognize as fact. The occult has a special place in this discourse. People have been dealing with, trying to understand, and worshipping in the occult for thousands of years. We can imagine that at the beginning of recorded history when knowledge was thin, to say the least, many explanations for the physical world were attributed to the metaphysical for no other reason that knowledge was so sparse. It's more than likely that as time progressed and the collective knowledge of humankind increased and libraries grew in size, the occult took an increasingly smaller role in people's lives. However, even today, the occult owns a special place in humankind's understanding of what is not yet understood.

It seems to me that even more importantly than those

individual and distinct things that qualify as the occult—for instance, mental telepathy, life after death, witchcraft, telekinesis, zombies, vampires, satyrs, werewolves, and other mythical creatures—is the intersection of these things through the various disciplines they touch.

For instance, life after death is a topic of much discussion in the fields of science, religion, and spirituality. How to sort out what is nonsense and what is widely believed to be true is a difficult prospect. Noknowlogy rears its head in this discussion as a catch-all, bundling all the reasons that a subject moves from the occult to hard science. Of course, it has to do with the increase in knowledge in any one subject.

Consider this as an example. Tens of thousands of years ago, there were solar eclipses. There were then; there still are now. Without question, these were a terrifying experience for the humans who observed them. We can read the history and listen to the folklore that is passed down about what the ancients thought and how they reacted to these events. These were in the realm of the occult. As soon as Galileo and Keppler had these phenomenon understood and explained by observation and mathematics, the solar eclipse moved from the occult into hard science. That meant that the tribes that sacrificed their livestock to appease the displeased God of the Sun were wasting their time and livestock.

Understanding that move from occult to hard science, let's think about another occult conundrum, mental telepathy. There are those who think that those who hold this phenomenon out as a certainly are looney, from the Latin word *Luna* from those who bay at the moon like a rabid wolf and have lost their senses. Is it not possible that these people are in the same position as the flat-earthers or those who ridiculed Galileo? Is it not possible or even likely that there is something along the lines of Einstein's fabric of gravity that envelopes us all and transmits telepathic information around the globe and even to the far reaches of space to humans and animals? How emotionally close do we get to our house pets? How intuitive are those animals? The anecdotal evidence is astounding when we are talking about the bonds between animals and humans as well as the bonds between humans. These bonds may well know no bounds.

Do we write this off completely based on what we know in 2018, or do we consider that noknowlogy provides for a chance, perhaps a sizeable or small opportunity, that in centuries from now we will gain an understanding of something unknown now but obvious then that will explain the now unexplainable? It's noknowlogy once more.

This brings to mind another group's long-lost recollections from a subsequent trip back to Singapore and its relationship to the occult. We were in the middle of a shipyard period at the same yard, the same facilities, in the early 1990s. It's strange how those voyages often blend into one. However I should start at the beginning.

Many years before then, I had a good friend and shipmate named Andy Wilson, a second-generation Pole from a coal mining family in West Virginia. I asked him one time how a fellow who lived and thought so obviously a Polish identity had a name like Wilson. He told me that when his grandfather came through Ellis Island, the immigration officer asked him what his name was. He replied Mikhail Wilkon.

The officer licked the nib of his quill pen and wrote carefully after dipping it in ink, "Michael Wilson."

"Your new name is Michael Wilson," he reported.

And that was how the Wilson family started their American experience, like many others did as well. But that is clearly another story altogether.

Andy was a swell guy and a really good sailor, shipmate, and friend. I was sailing on another ship as second mate when we heard the news that he had been killed in a fall from the superstructure of another vessel. That was a tremendous and heartbreaking loss to everyone who knew him, many who didn't know him, and, of course, his wife and five-year-old son.

It was a tragedy. He had been painting the superstructure

from a bosun's chair suspended by a rope, an ordinary day at sea for an experienced sailor like Andy. What they did not know at the time and what the investigation later revealed was that the steel railings that he secured his rope to were not steel at all. For some unknown reason, they were aluminum that had been joined to other steel rails. The joined-yet-dissimilar metals in the saltwater environment weakened the aluminum, and when Andy put his weight on the bosun's chair, the railing broke. He fell sixty-five feet onto a steel deck.

The ship was at sea at the time of the accident. The third mate on watch on the bridge was looking forward out the window as Andy fell. He swears that their eyes met and Andy instinctively reached out to him for help. That youngster was not the same after that grisly incident. There was nothing but rudimentary first aid available, and Andy passed away only a few minutes after falling. It was a tragedy.

Not long after Andy's death, strange things began to happen on that vessel. Time and time again, we heard the same story for many years following the accident. Andy had always worn denim overalls, work boots, a red flannel shirt, and a knitted blue watch cap. He had a full graying beard.

The story was always the same. Some new crew member would be taking a 2:00 a.m. coffee break in the crew's mess hall. A fellow would come in wearing a watch cap, a red flannel shirt, and denim coveralls. He wouldn't say a word. He would just walk through the crew mess hall. He might stop and look at the coffee pot. He would never face anybody there. He would never speak to anybody, and he would walk out the forward door and disappear.

The new crew member would ask his watch partners who that guy was. They would tell him it was the ghost of Andy Wilson, who had been killed in a fall aboard that ship a number of years before.

This went on for years and years. It was always the same story. Some people were understandably uneasy; others, like me, wanted to have a face-to-face with the ghost and catch up, if possible, with my old friend. I thought it was at least worth a try. I would say that this happened more than several times a year for probably ten or twelve years, so there were dozens of sightings.

At Jurong Shipyard in Singapore, they have lots of laborers working in the yard from places like Sri Lanka, Borneo, Palau, and Java. We came to work one morning at 8:00 a.m. to see our entire labor force standing on the quay. That was odd. Normally they would already be climbing aboard at this time. No work means no pay in foreign shipyards. It's a rough life for the workers. Benefits for the workers ... Flush toilets. They worked under difficult conditions for low pay.

Apparently the night watchman, an Indian fellow, had approached one of the company's contractors and asked him about the strange American in the watch cap and red shirt who had walked by him in the middle of the night and would not stop when asked who he was and what he was doing aboard. The guard had been getting a cup of coffee in the crew's mess when the apparition appeared.

The contractor, in a cavalier way, told the guard, "That must have been the ghost of Andy Wilson. He haunts the ship, and we see him from time to time. Perfectly nice chap he is. No worries about him at all. He just haunts the vessel!"

Apparently the watchman's eyes got as big as saucers, and he was gone in a flash, down the gangplank and up the quay in the shortest of order. The news of the haunted vessel spread faster than a wildfire. No worker would set foot on the vessel.

Not having any experience with this type of thing, I called the shipyard manager's office and spoke directly to him. He told me that the workers were all very superstitious and that the ship would have to undergo an exorcism before work could resume. *All right, an exorcism*, I thought. That was a first for me, but somehow I wasn't surprised. The sea captain gig is really a wonderful string of unusual and often odd life experiences.

The director asked if I had any ghost money aboard the vessel. I said no, not knowing what ghost money was. He said that was all right because we could go up to one of the spiritual shops, attached to one of the many temples in town, and buy some ghost money for the exorcism.

I also found out that we needed a Buddhist priest to be the officiant or the ceremony wouldn't be official. And we required some type of vessel or metal apparatus to contain a fire. We spent several hours getting all this together.

The Buddhist priest arrived in a cab, which amused me to no end for reasons I still can't figure out. Do exorcists really take a cab to an exorcism? Are they yellow cabs or metro cabs? Are exorcists good tippers to cabbies? Do they engage the cabbie in conversations regarding the number of wickets made at the cricket matches downtown across from Raffles?

The exorcist/priest wore long pastel-colored robes and Air Jordans. He was as bald as a cue ball and had designer frames on his glasses. Good money in exorcising ghosts, I guessed. I distinctly remember the unlicensed sailor's union representative, Jersey Tom, ask me in the middle of all this if the unlicensed crew would get overtime for attending an exorcism or penalty time, a contractual stipend for working under various abnormal conditions.

I think I answered him more with the look on my face than the verbal reply I remember giving him, which was, "Son, please take a minute to find the section in the union contract that applies to exorcisms of haunted vessels. When you find that, we'll get together and discuss it, and I'll make sure the matter receives all the attention it deserves."

This was getting surreal. When the time came to perform the ceremony, we had an assemblage of workers, management, and crew on board. We were midships on the weather deck. The chief engineer started a fire with diesel oil in a cut-down fifty-five-gallon drum. It was there on the main deck I recall the black smoke swirling upwards.

The priest started with several incantations and opened up a thick package of the brightly printed ghost money, which for all the world looks just like Monopoly money, only larger. He began to drop the ghost money into the flames. He chanted more incantations. Pieces of burning ghost money floated up on the rising air from the fire, reminding me of autumn leaves in northern New England in October, something I hadn't seen for a long, long time.

The exorcist then handed some more ghost money out to the others who were there observing the ceremony. They burned their ghost money too. I tried to pay attention to the words he was saying, but it was a lost cause. The priest then broke out this device that looked like a baby rattle with strings. When he twirled it, it made a rhythmic sound. When all the ghost money was gone, the priest looked up to the heavens and solemnly declared the vessel ghost-free.

It was like someone threw a switch. In minutes, swarms of happy shipyard workers overran us. And when it was done, the priest wanted to be paid in Marlboro cigarettes, not cash. He wanted genuine American Marlboros, the ones in the hard box, the ones that American ships carried. There were no soft packs for this exorcist. You can't make this up.

Now, company regulations specifically prohibited the proffering of what is known to people who deal on this level as *baksheesh* for services rendered or special treatment or favors anywhere in the world for any reason. It was simply not done in this Fortune 500 company. It was a first-order violation of the ethics policy and a firing offense.

The problem was that the policy authors never spent much—any—time on a haunted ship tied to a wharf in Singapore, managed by not a single person who had any kind of degree in petroleum engineering from LSU or any of the other wellheads of oil company upper management. This matter was beyond the realm of business ethics and sat squarely on pragmatism. The locker room at the River Oaks Golf Club in Houston was certainly as close to Southeast Asia and the real world of getting a job done as any of those folks had ever been.

So our priest got his Marlboros in the hard pack, in short order. I was later asked if I were going to write a report to headquarters regarding the exorcism.

My reply was, "And the point of that would be …?"

I did, however, make an entry in the Coast Guard's official log of this occurrence during a foreign voyage. "While in dry dock in Jurong Shipyard, Singapore, this day," the entry read, "vessel exorcised by Buddhist priest by methodology of burning of ghost money. Fire watch manned. Chief engineer and vessel's master in attendance. Vessel fully inspected. No evidence at this time of any remaining ghosts, spirits, or apparitions."

If I had that log today, I'd have already had it put up behind glass on the walls of the world-famous Gaspar's Grotto in Ybor City so guests might enjoy it.

As an interesting aside, it's now thirty-plus years later from those events, and I still keep my own personal stash of ghost money at home just in case I might need it. One never knows.

And Andy Wilson? He continued to show himself for years to come on a regular basis. So much for the actual efficacy of burning ghost money. After the vessel was broken up for scrap on a Mumbai mudflat years later, I wondered, and still do, where Andy's ghost went. Maybe a séance is in order some evening. Perhaps I'll take the lovely Mrs. S to the towns surrounding the Mumbai mudflats in search of an encounter with my dearly departed friend's ghost. If anybody could find him, it's me. I know well the kind of places he used to hang out in. So to me at least, it's clear that the occult is never that far away.

I'm willing to bet dollars to doughnuts that love is the singlemost studied, recorded, and thought about subject on the planet and in recorded history. I retract that. I think eating is first. Love runs a close second. Point of fact, a brilliant and gifted lyricist once wrote, "Love is all there is." I could argue that point to be argumentative, but we all know that's mostly true. If it's an organism with consciousness, it's probably seeking love twenty-four hours a day. Love binds the world together. It's a feeling we all know that's hard to describe. But you sure know it when you're in love. Most of us would agree that the more love there is, the better. The less love there is, the worse. This applies to everything and everybody and seems to be a universal truth, one that can't be argued with. The sun comes up in the east every day. Love on earth is good. It's an obvious truth, one of only a few. Simple, right?

But how simple is it? Do we even know what it is? Do we acknowledge that there is a lot we do know about love but there is probably a lot more that we do not know about love?

Who, having suffered a broken heart, could argue? How could something so wonderful only ten minutes before become so hurtful and destructive only minutes after a rejection? It happens all the time, a common occurrence. It sure hurts like hell, doesn't it?

From this observance, you could assume that love is a drug. Could you not? Sharing love with a person feels great. Having that love withdrawn results in immediate and nearly unbearable withdrawal pains in an overwhelming number of situations.

So what is love? It's an emotion. It's an electrical file generated by neurons, stored in the protoplasm of fatty brain cells of animals producing endorphins and other hormones. I really don't know a damn thing about it, but that sounds correct, does it not?

I could go on and on, parroting scores of books, verses, and theories about what love is and isn't. Try as I might, I probably couldn't do a shadow of the job that others who have concentrated on this, the most concentrated upon subject of all, have already done.

Consider this as a remote possibility. No human has ever been further away from a human they love than from the distance to the back side of the moon than from the surface of the earth. Someday, possibly soon, as interstellar space travel and time interact, we will be light-years from our loved ones. Will that make a difference? Will gravity waves that Einstein postulated turn out to be love waves? Is there a natural force that propels love across distance? Does absence really make the heart grow fonder?

Is there a physical reason for that, or is that patently absurd? Does love reside as a memory and only a memory? Is it a collection of electrons spanning a few synapses in the electrical fields of our brain, as sometimes revealed in Boolean photography? Certainly that is something possible too. We just don't know. How vain it would be to think that we in the twenty-first century were to actually have a full and complete understanding of such matters? We are vain, foolish, and consumed by ego. It's not a combination leading to "wise" by any stretch, is it?

The point I want to make about love is simply this: It is one of the most studied, observed, desired, and written about topics on the planet. You can safely assume it always has been and always will be. What is the theme of every—I exaggerate—popular music title ever recorded, except surfing and cars? The answer is love. Everything we know about this most important of all subjects is just anecdotal.

Where is the science? There must be a science. Why? We still don't know even a fraction of what is to be uncovered on the subject in the future. Perhaps in the future love will become a hard science. Instead of writing love songs, sonnets, and poems, professors of love will have huge blackboards of formulas and calculations attempting to prove various theorems concerning love. Earnest young graduate students with scruffy beards and horn-rimmed glasses will spend late nights in laboratories, titrating chemical compounds in elaborate distillation equipment in search of *it*. Who could bet against that based on the progress we have seen in the past recent decades in every other field? It's noknowlogy again.

CHAPTER 5

Lorenco Marques, Portuguese East Africa, 1973

Steven Choo was third mate on the *MorMac Pride*, a really swell old C-3 general cargo vessel with hydraulic winches, refrigerated tween decks, a swimming pool, and a certification to carry twelve passengers for hire. Built in the early 1950s at Sun Shipbuilding in Pennsylvania, it was the first ship I was ever paid to sail on. I was a nineteen-year-old deck cadet and an officer in training, and the venerable Merchant Marine Act of 1936 specified I was to receive $1.37 a day as pay, if I'm remembering correctly, to which there is some doubt. If I'm wrong, it's by cents, not by dollars.

Steven lived in the cabin across the passageway from mine. His cabin had a porthole; mine did not. He was a union sailor, MMP, Master's Mates and Pilots, as I recall. That is a book in itself. He was of Chinese descent, about forty years old. He stood about five-feet nothing and spoke almost unrecognizable English in the heaviest possible Chinese accent. He was a reprobate of the highest order.

Regarding the most serious vices, he had them all, in spades. He didn't miss a one—drank, smoked, cheated, womanized, fought, gambled, stole, and lied. Do I leave any out? And those are only the ones I actually witnessed. He was my mentor, and I idolized the man I wanted to be just like him. He was the man who taught me to break out the Beefeaters London Dry Gin whenever the ship approached the equator. Open the bottle; throw away the cap. You weren't going to need that cap again.

"Keeps malaria away," he would say.

I only found out later it was the quinine in the tonic that was effective against malaria. Had I known, I wouldn't have argued anyway. Steven was swell with me. I was nineteen years old while the average age of the ship's crew, including me, was sixty-three. So anybody who would even give me the time of day was a fast friend. It can be lonely at sea, riding steel ships for a living.

Steven was also the man who taught me how to stay safe while coming back to the ship from a night of drinking and carousing through the most dangerous and deserted streets on the world's roughest waterfronts, often alone and sometimes half in the bag. These were places where even the rats weren't safe and knew enough to avoid.

We were in a bar called the New York Bar in Lorenco Marques, Mozambique, East Africa, in the early 1970s. No lie, there were young kids of thirteen and fourteen wearing ragtag quasi-military uniforms with well-oiled submachine guns slung over their shoulders. All of them smoked up on the local equivalent of Ghanja. It was scary business. There were working girls … working. There were gamblers, touts and drug dealers, beggars, pimps, and lots of sailors. The oft-referenced bar scene in *Star Wars* had nothing on the New York Bar in what is now known as Maputo. (I recently learned of its name change. I'm still more comfortable with Lorenco Marques than Maputo as well as Bombay than Mumbai and the Belgium Congo to Zaire. Maybe someday the politicians will change the name of New York City to Gotham City or Pleasanton. But I digress.)

I do remember vividly the beer we were drinking to excess. It was called Laurentina, and I understand that it's still available in country. In actuality, many South Africans take the drive north from Durban, S.A., specifically for that purpose. But that too is another story altogether.

It was late, time to go back to the ship, get a nap, and then go on watch. Steven ordered us both two Laurentinas from the bartender, a stunningly tall young woman, black as coal wearing short shorts and a bikini top. I remember her midriff. Someone had used a sharp instrument to cut her skin in small dots. Perhaps *puncture* is a better word. It must have taken hours, but like its cousin, the tattoo, the resultant body art in scar tissue was unreal. She was, as I said, black as coal, but the scars were pink. She wore this scar picture of a round grass hut with a thatched roof. Zulu, I think. Round huts in Southeast Africa are always Zulu. And, I suppose, that's where her height came from. The hut was in a village. Outside the hut was a loin-clothed man with a spear. He was defending himself from an attacking male lion. The entire front of her abdomen from under her breasts to just above her beltline was this artwork. It was all in scar tissue. It was like a train wreck. You didn't want to look, but you just had to. I've never seen anything like it or since.

"What's your name?" I asked.

"Maria." She smiled back at me with near-perfect teeth as we shook hands over the bar.

I wondered about the practice and availability of dentistry in Mozambique, as opposed to great genetics. I never came to any conclusions on that matter. Strange thoughts.

One beer came across the bar already open, and another remained capped. There were no twist-off caps in those days. Men were men and would often open them with their teeth or bare hands.

I inquired, "What's the deal with the beers?"

Steven said in his thickest Chinese-accented English, "We going back to ship, right? Verry baad baad neighborhood, right? So order two beers."

He was a little bit in the bag, slurring his words and right up in my face, mind you. I smelled the garlic from the Indian Ocean shrimp he had eaten earlier. Not good.

"Open one and drink it going home. The other one, the full one, goes in back pocket. All the way to the ship, you walk right down middle of street. Anybody steps off curb, you take beer out of your pocket, hold it by neck, and smash it on the street. Railroad tracks is best. Stand up. Hold out the broken beer bottle. Let them see it. If your hand bleeding, that better. They hear and see that ... ain't nobody gonna mess with you!"

As he said this last line, he spoke very slowly, carefully, and in a singsong cadence, wagging his right index finger back and forth in front of my astonished face, like a metronome, for punctuation. He squinted his eyes as he got chin to chin with me, nodding his head and grinning maniacally. He burped. Garlic.

That was forty-five years ago, and all the subsequent times I've had the wife and family to South America, Europe, Asia, Africa, and the Middle East, I've never finished a night out without unobtrusively and nearly unconsciously, taking a full, capped longneck back to wherever we were going at the end of the night, snug in my back pocket.

Over all those years, I've reached for that back-pocket beer on only a few occasions for reassurance. I've broken the bottle once, maybe twice, if only to gain attention, but I have never had to brandish one in anger. Thank the Lord. Old habits, well-learned, die hard. Nobody has ever questioned the method. You can't. It works. I have, however, given to many a young sailor, innumerable sailors in fact, the same lesson given to me by my good friend, Third Mate Steven Choo, that night in the New York Bar in Lorenco Marques, Mozambique, in 1973. It turns out Steven, through his good work in this matter, has benefited humankind.

He would be pleased and amused to know that he could be called a humanitarian!

Recently a lifelong merchant ship's captain and childhood friend, Wild Bob, meandered into a spot in Cape Town, South Africa, where he should have known better not to go. If you're looking for trouble, you normally don't have to look very hard to find some. There, he encountered three hoods bent on relieving him of his cash. Three had never previously been an unreasonable number for my friend Wild Bob to deal with. Regardless of that, he ended up with a deep knife wound on his left scapular. Literally he was stabbed in the back. It could have been his throat. He admits he's lucky to be alive. Age catches up to all of us (if you're lucky). Apparently it took a long time to heal, and he had an unhappy and substantial bit of explaining to do to the vessel's ownership. Normally ship owners take a dim view of such things where their captains are involved. It's dicey business. I like to think that Steven Choo's beer bottle procedure might have saved him all those homemade stitches put in by his ship's bosun.

In the arts, music in particular, many composers, songwriters, and musicians make it a point to use the "rest" or silence in their compositions or performances of various works. It's a part of the fabric and vernacular of many types of music. The silence offsets or perhaps punctuates the notes that are actually played—amplifying them, accenting them, changing them, and even highlighting them. Deft use of silence is what often sets apart outstanding music from ordinary pieces.

In the visual arts, take painting and drawing as an example. The outlines and masses formed by drawing leave a phenomenon known as negative space. That space balances the forms. You simply cannot put one down on a canvas or sketch pad without producing the other.

If you drew a chair on a piece of paper, the negative space is everything else on that paper with the exception of the chair. If you want to focus on that negative space and repeat to copy the negative space onto another paper, you would see a drawing of a chair even though you didn't intend to draw a chair.

So it is with noknowlogy. All the knowledge and ideas we acquire is encircled by the infinite possibilities of what we do not know. It seems that the finite amount of knowledge that we are on a quest to acquire only leads to an indication that there is so much more in the infinite realm of what is unknown. It's curious. Doesn't this sound like space exploration?

The contention here is that noknowlogy may turn out to be a useful tool. In the 1600s, Isaac Newton did not have the needed mathematics to solve complicated problems that were presenting themselves to a society becoming increasingly less agrarian while the industrial revolution was gaining steam (yes, pun intended). So he invented what is known today as The calculus. The study of calculus today produces brilliant and elegantly simple solutions to complex problems with many constantly changing variables. It's so brilliant in fact that when the answer pops out of the worksheet, it feels like witchcraft. It is a discipline that you either understand or don't understand. In the field of engineering and other hard sciences, it has become indispensable.

Newton didn't have the tools, so he made them. Perhaps noknowlogy will allow us to examine other fields. After all, have we not previously decided that you can't know what you don't know?

CHAPTER 6

Somewhere off the west coast of the USA, early 1980's

I'd been sailing this old tank vessel as chief mate/relieving master for several years back in 1981–1986, up and down the West Coast of the United States as far north as Alaska and as far south as Hawaii. I'd make an occasional shipyard trip to the Far East, Singapore, and Korea. And there'd be an occasional trip to Panama's west coast. We spent a lot of time in San Francisco, and there wasn't much that could surprise me about the crew members that we had aboard who were native to there.

The early 1980s were rough. We lost a lot of friends, neighbors, and shipmates to HIV/AIDS in those dangerous years. Everybody was shell-shocked and fatalistic. There was more bad news coming out on almost a daily basis and few answers. Most everyone you met was terrified. I had a Haitian sailor aboard who thought he was going to get AIDS just because he was Haitian. No lie. Rumors were rampant, and nobody knew anything for sure, except that friends were dying at an increasing rate. Those of us who were there at the time were witness to a genuine and very real panic.

One of my best sailors was Bobby Van Pelt, an extremely flamboyant sort who looked like the hard-hat guy in Village People and acted that way too. But that was him. He'd been through a lot and no longer made any bones about who or what he was.

I asked him one time, "What was the most important thing you learned from your father?"

"He taught me what it was like to get punched in the face by a full-grown man."

How do you respond to a tragedy like that? He fit right in with my bunch because no matter who we were, we all got along and really enjoyed each other. I never had to ask for that approach to camaraderie or mutual respect from that gang. They just wanted to live, work, and get along. Sailors are good like that. In Bobby's case, it also helped that he was a hell of a talented sailor and a really nice human being. He was as naturally funny in a sardonic sort of way as they come.

We normally had two able seaman and an ordinary seaman on every four-hour long watch. Known as watch partners, they worked together every day for months and invariably formed a tight bond.

Bobby's watch partner was Gerhardt, who couldn't have been much more different than Bobby if we had handpicked them. An ex–Navy Seal, Gerhardt stood about six-foot-two and weighed 250 rock-hard pounds. He had a thirty-two-inch waist and a chest resembling a beer barrel. He had a big walrus moustache and biceps any blacksmith would have to envy. Picture a huge Yosemite Sam, bandy-legged and all. Picture Brock Lesnar with long hair and a moustache.

Gerhardt came from Alabama and had that Southern accent to round out the effect. He was the toughest, most capable man I ever knew. He said BUDS, SEALS basic training, was the most fun he ever had. He was the kind of man who had no difficulty at all in walking away from trouble because he had absolutely nothing to prove to himself or anyone else. That was Gerhard.

He and Bobby got along great and shared a mutual respect except for the verbal jabs they often threw at one another in order to keep their relationship neither too close nor distant. Their practical joking was an essential part of their relationship. It was one thing that these two very different breeds of cats could comfortably bond over.

We tied up one afternoon not far from San Francisco, well up the bay. It wasn't going all that well. The ballet of ships, tugboats, line boats, line handlers, sailors, monkey fists, and heaving lines was not flowing for any particular reason. None of this is rocket science, but there are many moving parts. Few of the moving parts were moving harmoniously that afternoon, resulting in lots of extra work and time for everybody. Normally, it all came together seamlessly, but not that afternoon.

Gerhardt, usually unflappable after a life full of difficult and dangerous experiences rolling off his back like water off a duck, was actually getting testy. I looked down from the bridge at him and Bobby toe to toe, and neither looked happy. I later found out what was said as Gerhardt pushed Bobby away and elbowed his way into where Bobby was working with a very heavy synthetic rope.

Apparently he had said in his thickest ex–Navy Seal Southern drawl, "Son, why don't you get a job you can actually do, like hairdresser?"

He began throwing the heavy line back and forth across a pair of huge iron mooring bits by himself. That was crossing the line, and Bobby was staring daggers at his watch partner and then turning on his heel.

Several days later, we were back out to sea. The ship was rolling slowly and heavily as we were heading north to pick up another load of crude oil. Huge, rolling Pacific swells were very long, as they tend to get when generated by mid-Pacific storms thousands of miles to the west. She shuddered just a bit as she changed direction and then would accelerate back through the roll … over and over and over again. If you were a type who suffered from motion sickness, it would not have been a good day for you.

We were all out there just doing our part to keep the lights on and the cars running in California. Somebody found me at my desk in my sea cabin just behind the bridge and across from the gyro compass room and told me that Gerhardt was sick. I grabbed my medical bag and headed down to the crew's quarters to find Gerhard in his focs'l, sprawled across his bunk looking very pale. (focs'l is short for forecastle, that part of the vessel where the crew was quartered.) Clammy is a better word.

I turned up his light, hooked the focs'l door back, and asked him what was going on. He told me he was light-headed and had chest pains and pain in his left shoulder and arm. He also complained of dizziness and sweatiness. So instantly I'm thinking the same thing he is, a heart attack. This is a bad scene when not even a long-range helicopter oftentimes cannot get a patient off a heavily rolling ship hundreds of miles out to sea.

Years before I had gone to medical school of sorts. I was training there, way up in Maine, with old Doc Smythe to be the ship's doctor. My medical training, soup to nuts, had lasted a full three weeks. There was neither a statutory requirement nor an immediate necessity to put a real doctor on a merchant ship carrying less than twelve passengers crewed by twenty-five to thirty fairly young and middle-aged, mostly healthy men. So they trained us up for three weeks, deemed us amply prepared, and put us back on our ships with a heartfelt "best of luck."

Occasionally someone passed away. It was inevitable. It was a known fact that if you had a medical emergency, you were not getting the same care you would ashore. It's not even close. It's another reason we were well paid. There was always that risk. People died on ships from heart attacks, strokes, blood clots, and hot appendixes all the time. It was just part of the life.

The company we worked for subscribed to a service where we

could get medical advice from an actual doctor, the kind whose medical school took considerably longer than three weeks, via the radio 24-7. Their offices were located outside of Washington DC, and our single sideband transceiver was equipped with a 1,000-watt amplifier, which was plenty of power to get from the middle of the Gulf of Alaska to KHT, the commercial radio station we used that was located in Cedar Rapids, Iowa. They would then patch us into the phone lines, and we would have our doctor in Washington.

Nothing is simple at sea. These were in the days before satellite telephones, of course. That afternoon I ran up and down the five stories of ladders on the ship that were between Gerhard's quarters and the radio room more times than I could count. I thought I might be the one needing medical attention next.

So I was sitting on the corner of Gerhardt's bunk, taking his blood pressure again, which was still high. I was doing my best to keep the patient calm. The radio doctor was hoping there was just a panic attack here. If we were lucky, perhaps.

Still, Gerhardt was scared stiff, talking an awful lot about his mom and how sorry he was he was such a jerk to her as a kid. I thought, *Calm. Steady. Calm. Keep him calm. Do what the doctor says. Administer the medication. Relax.*

Bam! Crash! Into the room burst Bobby. He screeched to a stop.

He said in a loud, clear voice with all the possible hand gesturing and flamboyance he could muster, "Captain, oh, Captain! I cleaned out that large corner space on the floor in the FROZEN MEAT LOCKER just the way you told me to!"

He turned to Gerhardt as if Gerhardt hadn't heard any of that, and feigning surprise, he said, "Oh! Hi, Gerhardt. Hope you're feeling better!" and finger-waved with a "Toodles."

Bobby pranced out the door, as pleased as he could be with his performance as Gerhardt turned as white as the sheets and started to shake and hyperventilate, now entering that full-blown panic attack. He began to sob.

Of course I had never told Bobby to do any such thing. He just felt that reminding Gerhardt of what happened to sailors who passed away at sea would be ample retribution for Gerhard's prior "hairdresser" crack. And he was more than right. I will say that Bobby gave as good as he got. And although it wasn't funny at the time, it turned out to be one of my most told sea stories. Gerhardt is still living, last I heard. Bobby, on the other hand, passed years ago to the "illness." Only the good die young. Rest in peace, young man.

Early into this twenty-first century, humans have made tremendous advances in the field of biology. There are no arguments there. The tools of technology provide quantifiable and verifiable amounts of data on all types of organisms (from the word *organic*, which is "carbon bearing") from elephants to sugar ants and mold spores. Literally millions and millions of these organisms have been studied. But how many of them have not been? Has the study of these known organisms been completed? That is, has all there is to learn from them been learned? A better question is this: of all the organisms we know and have studied, are they all of the organisms? Hardly. New discoveries are being brought forward regularly, it seems.

And life, a little carbon, a little water, a touch of hydrogen, a wee dram of oxygen, and a dash of amino acids add a spark. Poof! It's life. Not so fast. Has anybody ever made the nonliving alive. Not yet, aside from Dr. Frankenstein. We may have changed a few things in life, and that is no small accomplishment, but no one has ever made life. It's somewhere in the future … perhaps. But who is to know?

And that is the point. No clearer example of what we don't know is the rapidly increasing body of knowledge that makes up the science of biology. Scientists are mucking around with molecules for heaven's sakes. It is obvious, although unprovable, that the body of unknown knowledge in the field of biology grows twofold, fourfold, sixfold, or whichever to every breakthrough discovery in that same field. It's noknowlogy.

Consider the sugar ant. A dozen such creatures can live on the head of a pin. We take them for granted and treat them as a nuisance. But they really are a miracle, nothing less. They're so small you need a microscope to examine them. Each is a highly evolved micro-miniature biological chemical plant contained in a biological nanomachine.

Think for a moment about what they are and are fully equipped to do:

- They live, a full-blown miracle all by itself, if one is inclined to believe in miracles.
- They eat, processing food into energy for their survival.
- They forage in order to eat.
- They breathe, using oxygen in a chemical process to produce life-sustaining energy.
- They move. Muscles propel them through tiny ligaments, joints, and skeletal structures.
- They think. There are tiny brains there, a hundred times smaller than the period ending this sentence.
- They defend themselves.
- They flee.
- They reproduce their species, not a bit less remarkable than any other biological reproduction.
- They cooperate, building communal tunnels and living in communities.
- Because they cooperate, they must—and do—communicate.

What are the chances that our most modern nanotechnology could produce such a miraculous machine? Zero. Not yet. Not even if it were to weigh five hundred pounds and be the size of a car, never mind a ten-thousandth of a gram. Perhaps someday but certainly not yet. They're smaller than a grain of sand and so impossibly complex that it has more in common with humans than we might recognize.

If all this is true, there has to be a point to be made here. That will come as we proceed. Patience, please.

CHAPTER 7

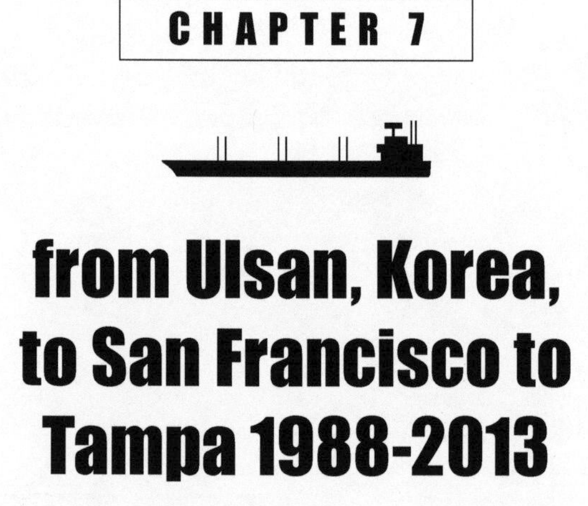

from Ulsan, Korea, to San Francisco to Tampa 1988-2013

So, it was 2013, I guess. I was sitting on a barstool in the world-famous Gaspar's Grotto, a well-known, iconic and much-loved watering hole in Ybor City, Tampa, Florida. It's a mashup of every bar that I've been to on all the continents scattered all over the globe. People use words like *magical* and *special*. We agree. If you haven't been there and are a fan of special people, places, and treatment, then you should treat yourself and go there. Make the pilgrimage to this one-of-a-kind shrine to humanity, alcohol, and fellowship. You won't be sorry. No, sir. Never sorry.

Gaspar's Grotto is only a few blocks away from the shipyard and the Port of Tampa. The bar was full of working men and the women who didn't mind them much. People were drinking "the special," which consisted of a shot of whiskey of dubious pedigree and a short beer, all for the princely sum of two dollars. (The price has gone up. Now it's two shots and two beers for five dollars.)

I was sitting next to a fellow wearing a yellow jumpsuit, couple of grease stains, well-worn leather boots, and a dog-eared notebook in his top pocket. He had a British accent, as it turned out. I was putting it together. What was my take? This fellow had flown in from someplace within twenty-five miles to the north of London, on contract to a steamship line for his marine engineering expertise. He was working at a ship in the shipyard. I was guessing all of this, but it was written all over him as "shipyard repair superintendent." I've known dozens of these fellows and always enjoyed the time I spent with them. They're solid guys, working men, just another subculture of the marine business. All of us together make up a bunch of queer ducks, but that's what makes it interesting.

So I asked him the question I already knew the answer to. "Working at the yard?"

He said, "Yes."

Of course. It turns out I'd hit the nail on the head with him. I could have written his life story, and he probably could have written mine! We continued to talk and drink, and the subject got around to foreign shipyards.

And I said to him," I took the *Explorer Beaumont* into Hyundai Mipo Shipyard in Ulsan, Korea, back in 1988."

He remarked, "I was there too that year. Small world!"

We drank to that. So in a collegial spirit, fueled by further spirits, I delivered this intricate sea story to him. He seemed interested.

I explained to my new friend, "So there we are, coming alongside the pier at Hyundai Mipo Shipyard with the *Beaumont* shortly after arrival at Ulsan, Korea, in June 1988. It's a driving rain. Soaked-to-the-bone wind is blowing a gale. We get her made fast with no further problems. As the riggers are putting up the gangways, the shipyard crane swings a bunch of our contractors in a personnel box over the rail and onto the main deck. These are the folks who will help get the work done safely and efficiently. They work for the ship owner. Some are contractors; others are employees. None are crew members. The repair inspector, Jackson, throws a leg over the box. We have all worked together intermittently for years on similar repair periods. This is going to be easy. He gets out and starts up the long trek to the bridge, where I'm having a cup of coffee with the chief engineer. Meetings will get formal soon so we can have an informal one right now.

"Jackson, the repair inspector, comes onto the bridge. Soaking wet, he shakes hands all around and grabs a steaming cup of coffee. We share a few pleasantries and some derogatory comments about the quality of this shipyard's work, the food in town, the Korean culture, including the odd odor a human body emanates when kimchi is eaten at every meal of every day, and the state of male-female relations in Ulsan, particularly as it impacts visiting male foreign nationals, all the topics shipyard folks and sailors need to talk about.

"Jackson says, 'Okay, Chief, Captain … you see that?' He points out the bridgewing door into the swirling downpour. 'See what?' we asked. 'Those guys are over there spray-painting the freaking *Trans Seas New York* in the freaking rain,' Jackson points out.

"And sure enough, right across the pier from us, these two Korean painters, high up in a hydraulic cherry picker, are spray-painting the side of this huge vessel in the rain. They are suspended forty feet above the pier on a hydraulic lift, blowing tens of thousands of dollars of time and material into the soggy maelstrom, at high pressure, to no possible gain or effect.

"Jackson continues, 'This is what you are going to get here, lousy work. Unless we stay on top of this job, they'll give the ship a cheap shave and a haircut, and that will be the result. Then we'll all have to live with it for another two years.' He pointed to the painters.

"So my chief engineer, a Down-easter from as far up in Maine as you can get and not be in Canada, perhaps it was Eastport, or Eastpot, as he would pronounce it, asks Jackson, 'Where are the chief, the captain, and the repair inspector? They're getting paid to make sure that doesn't happen.' You have to be familiar with a Down-easter's accent to really understand how that came out.

"Jackson pulls the three of us together like he's going to tell us a secret. Lowering his voice, he says, 'The chief, the captain, and the repair inspector are all on Cheju Do Island, a resort facility just off the coast. Been there for three days so far. They are there with two cases of Jack Daniels and six female escorts, not a one of them past their early twenties, rumor has it. Been gone for three days so far, I hear!' Jackson cleared his throat and rolled his eyes at *escorts*.

"He continued, 'The shipyard operations supervisor, Mr. Park, will be down here in less than an hour. He will ask you men if you've ever been to Cheju Do. And he'll also ask what your favorite whiskey is. I strongly suggest that you do not take him up on that generous invitation, not unless you want to have this ship painted in the rain.' He pointed over his shoulder with his thumb to the debacle taking place just across the pier.

"As it turned out, Mr. Park was truly perplexed why these seemingly normal American males didn't want to spend some time on Cheju Do with his female friends, having a drink or two and relaxing. It made no sense at all to him. Welcome to Far Eastern shipyards.

"Fast-forward ten months later, we are in San Francisco Bay, having completed that successful shipyard and sailing back across the Pacific in fifteen days to get the vessel back in service, carrying cargo, making money for the owners ... what we do. Things are going well, but the guys are still talking about the two cases of Jack Daniels and especially the six Korean escorts, two per man, whom in the telling and retelling of the story have now become just barely eighteen years old. My Lord! Things like that leave an impression on reprobate sailors, truth be told.

"We are in San Francisco Bay to discharge a load of Alaskan crude oil, passing the piers at Richmond, California, just before sunset one evening, and who is there? It's the *Trans Ocean New York*! This gets better. There is not one shred of paint along her entire 850-foot length. Plenty of orange primer, but not a chip of paint. It had all fallen off in sheets because she had been painted in the rain! We laughed like hell when we saw that. Our sides hurt we laughed so hard. I explained it to the San Francisco pilot who was aboard at the time, taking the ship up to the dock, and he roared too."

Fast-forward again, twenty-five more years to this ex–sea captain in the present day, who was now firmly moored to his barstool at the world-famous Gaspar's Grotto in Tampa. He was having a conversation about a 1988 shipyard in Ulsan, Korea, with another fellow who apparently was there simultaneously. He was telling this gentleman about an offered trip to Cheju Do Island off the coast of Korea with two cases of Jack Daniels and a half-dozen young Korean female escorts. But there was a refusal to take the shipyard's management up on that most generous and compelling offer because we didn't want to get the ship painted in the rain like the *Trans Seas New York*.

About this time in Gaspar's Grotto in 2013, there was a light dawning in this retired captain's brain. This fellow he was talking to was turning red. He was shifting in his seat and clearing his throat. Looking down, he nervously looked back at me and said sheepishly, "Captain, that was me!"

You could have knocked me out of that barstool with a feather! Struck dumb by the coincidence, the only thing I could say was, "Small industry, isn't it?" Twenty-five years later on a barstool halfway around the world, it's a small world indeed.

I didn't have the nerve to ask him how old those escorts really were. He would have lied anyway!

CHAPTER 8

Ulsan, South Korea, 1989

You would think that with all the available modern tools of technology we would understand the planet on which we live. Certainly with orbiting satellites overhead pinpointing, within inches, the position of any object on the planet at any time, this has to be true. But really, how much do we know about our own planet?

Weather is perhaps the most consequential force on the planet. Weather is the science and study of our atmosphere. Many of the other hard sciences converge in the field of weather. Thermodynamics, fluid dynamics, physics, and chemistry all combine in the study of weather. Weather is the net result of all these disciplines.

The first thing most people do every day is check the weather, react to that observation by planning activities, and don protective clothing as needed. Weather controls our activities, movements, and safety, 24-7. For the most part, it is changing constantly. There are moment-to-moment, daily, weekly, seasonal, and long-term changes. All of these occur at the same time. There are layers of influential changes in the weather, which produce an end result that we measure, react to, and often record.

Weather controls our economic activity and even our survival on the planet. I would put forward that because of all the variables that continue to change at the same time and at different places and times, the weather is really never the same and nearly unpredictable. And the result is what we see from moment to moment and must react to. I would opine that far more people have been killed and injured by weather in human history than by any other cause.

Weather used to be an art: the interpretation of subtle changes in wind direction or strength, the changes in types of clouds, or changes in barometric pressure, for example. Even lack of change in barometric pressure can be an indicator, along with wind direction, of the movement of consequential air masses. The more instrumentation that has been developed over the decades, the less of an art that weather observation and forecasting has become. The ultimate tool now is the weather satellite that allows meteorologists the ability to watch air mass movement in real time. This makes forecasting considerably easier than when it was an art.

However, as in the example of a major hurricane, even though the meteorologists can see it and the surrounding air masses, both the intensity and track are difficult to predict, even a few hours out. It's all the changing variables, all happening at the same time, to varying and unpredictable degrees that makes this forecasting difficult. The more we learn about the weather, the more we learn that there is so much more to know. It's noknowlogy.

Let's consider the oceans. Scientists say that 98 percent of the world's oceans are unexplored. That's obviously a lot of territory using the size of the earth as your standard. And at miles deep with pressures so staggering at depth, no light, and frigid cold, there is no expectation that these areas will be explored any time soon. And once again, with every new discovery comes a myriad of questions. As far as the oceans are concerned, we know very little. Humans have drilled down only a few thousand feet into the crust of earth, again only to find the most inhospitable conditions of pressure and temperature. How did this occur? Do the shifting tectonic plates suggest we live on an old planet or a relatively new one? There are many theories about the genesis of the earth, but what do we know as fact? Aside from literal scratching of the surface, there is not much to be done. We are like chickens rooting around in the dirt for a grub. We continue to bring new tools to bear on these questions—deeper drills, ground-penetrating radar, and low-frequency radio waves. New data points are being recorded, but what does the data mean? Only theories are postulated. In other words, all we can do is think about these problems. This data is a most powerful tool, clearly, but in this discussion, it solves little and proves nothing.

Read any of the great number of books on the subject of magnetism. Each will explain that magnetism is an "attractive force." But what does that mean? Most of the women I dated back in the dark ages could be suitably described by "attractive force." How does magnetism work? Although recognized centuries ago and used in compasses, electrical-generating equipment, parlor tricks, and nifty devices and novelties ever since, all we know is how to use it. There is little understanding of what that "attractive force" actually is.

In the past several decades, further discoveries have been made in this field combining magnetism with cryogenics. Humans being humans, we quickly employed engineering to put the properties of superconduction to use in reducing the resistance of electrical flow to near zero and creating superefficient electrical and electronic devices. One would conclude that the use of this principle is actually more relevant than the science behind that principle. But again, once human beings have discovered a natural phenomenon, further discovery often grinds on at a slower rate because the discovery opens up a Pandora's box of new questions. The amount of new questions outpaces the resources to investigate these questions, leaving a larger and growing backlog of questions not yet answered.

If we have not passed the point already, there may soon be places where there are more questions waiting to be answered than people on earth possessing the ability, time, or even sheer numbers to answer them, not unlike the national debt of the United States of America, where its division among the population leaves a staggeringly large number still. At some point, the exponential growth of these numbers inhibits and then prohibits the reversal of the trend. This may well be another of the core principles of noknowlogy. These exercises in numbers in order to find natural principles are tremendously interesting. I'm sure a theoretical mathematician would have no trouble explaining why, but the rest of us are left to ponder the result of these either intricate and highly involved mathematical calculations or a staggering simple principle as easily understood as one plus one equals two. I'm not bright enough to know which.

But as an example of this, here's another parlor trick. Did you know that you cannot fold a single sheet of anything of any size in half, cleanly, more than seven times? You will want to bet considerable amounts of money on this proposition once you are convinced of its seemingly impossible truth. Try a sheet of paper or newsprint, a huge drop cloth, a tent, or the biggest flag in the NFL. You can't do it.

So that's the kind of natural principle that we can use (to amuse) without having to know the why behind it. Is it noknowlogy, witchcraft, or just a simple mathematical proposition that indicates that doubling any thickness seven times creates a sum of the doubled layers that, no matter how thin the layers, the number is too large to physically contend with? Or something along those lines … We know that a math wizard will have that understanding and explanation better than you or me, just regular folks.

Before leaving this discussion, let's look at one more natural phenomenon whose discovery has led to amazing engineering: nuclear physics. Only a hundred years or so ago, Madam Curie unknowingly sacrificed herself and her husband for humanity in her laboratory while exploring the properties of radium. It seems that people have always had a fascination with things that glow. I, on the other hand, was schooled early by an electrical engineering professor who told our class sagely, "If it's glowing blue, don't touch it." (He was referring to a 50,000-volt Klystron tube in a marine radar unit.) He was a smart fellow. I digress.

Professor Roentgen also sacrificed himself in his development of the x-ray tube. He unknowingly cooked his gizzard much to the detriment of his own earthly longevity. The discovery in the early 1940s under the bleachers at the University of Chicago that a critical mass once achieved could produce a chain reaction was the final piece of the puzzle. Technology was about to prove Albert Einstein right for the first but not last time. Thus the atomic bomb was born, along with nuclear submarines, nuclear electrical generation, and nuclear medicine. It's odd how weapons have always been the first use of newly discovered technology. The Bronze Age wasn't named for the widespread use of wonderfully exceptional bronze pen nibs or frying pans, was it? Early bronze was used in swords that held a superior edge while waylaying the enemy to change the course of history. Typical. Humans being humans. I have more on that later where it intersects with human development and psychology.

And speaking of human development, meet Torrance Burke, one of my sailors on the *Explorer Universe.* A nineteen-year-old college dropout from Seattle, he probably never had a chance in college, unless he was going to study gender studies or the social sciences in the twenty-first century, subjects that seem to be a melting pot for people who want to study and pay lots of money to get a degree in stupid. But that's another book entirely. Perhaps if I choose to write that book, I'll let it fly and tell you how I really feel regarding the state of those matters.

Torrance was actually a swell kid. He just wasn't bright. But he was funny and compassionate. A likeable sort, he did not have a mean bone in his body. I was sailing captain on this vessel and took a special interest in this fellow because—I don't remember why—he was a good kid who needed a chance and, if handled correctly, might develop into a solid citizen. I took him under my wing. My interest in him also kept anybody who felt like bullying him at bay. He was the kind of fellow who might attract those type of folk, as he was gentle, very naive, and a little silly.

We were sailing on a ship that was built to compete with the growing expansion of the American domestic petroleum pipeline business in the 1960s. Pipelines could only deliver their product to the other end of the pipeline. Ships, on the other hand, could deliver it to any city that had a pier, some tanks, and thirty-two feet of water depth. That was the only competitive advantage that ships held over pipelines. It has always been vastly more economical to operate a pipeline than a ship. Ships need people on duty all the time. Those people have to be paid. Pipelines lay buried as they transport oil. There are no people who have to be paid, as a practical matter.

The point is that because of the competitive economic disadvantage of these ships competing against a pipeline, the ships were designed and built inexpensively. As such, these ships had communal toilets and showers. These facilities were down the passageway from the cabins where the crew slept. This was not a problem in 1965. But in the 1980s when women were now beginning to be hired to crew these ships, there were some obvious obstacles to overcome. There's a lot to be said about the women-on-ships movement. I won't go further at this time than to say for the record that I have always supported it, except with only a few individuals and those for good reason. Perhaps we can explore that more later.

On this particular ship, one of Torrance's fellow crew members was a woman named Cynthia. Cynthia came out of a union school for unlicensed personnel in the Pacific Northwest. There was not a thing wrong with Cynthia. She was a good sailor and a fine person. That added up to a good shipmate. Her performance exuded confidence, with good reason, and that built trust. She had a dry sense of humor.

What made it even easier having Cynthia on board was that she was a lesbian. She was unapologetically "out," and she was well respected and equally and fairly treated in every case. She was one of the guys, so to speak. She was no different from the rest of us really because we were all a little different in one way or another.

So Torrance came out of the shower one day, carrying a bar of soap in a plastic box with a towel wrapped around his waist. A big puff of wet steam was behind him as the shower room door slammed shut. He headed aft toward his focs'l flip-flopping down the long, narrow, and dimly lit linoleum-covered passageway. His focs'l was one or two past Cynthia's.

Cynthia's door was open. She was sitting at her small folding wall desk, writing a letter home. A 40-watt incandescent bulb in the built-in desk lamp poured weak yellow light over her work. Torrance walked by in his flip-flops and towel and saw Cynthia. He stopped and turned. He said hello to Cynthia. Torrance was nothing if not affable.

She put down her pen and looked up. "Hello."

They were only six or eight feet apart. It was close quarters. Torrance was feeling pretty good. He was nineteen years old with a ripped six-pack. He was a good-looking reddish-blond kid, footloose and fancy free. So Torrance stepped onto her threshold and leaned against the door frame. He put his right hand behind his head, elbow on the door frame, and flexed his bicep. He tightened his abs for effect. He made a strong play for the attention of this woman as he ran his fingers through his luxurious, freshly washed mane, pursing his lips.

Witnesses to this uncomfortable scene said this was getting wildly out of control and fast. The funny part is that, Cynthia being Cynthia, she was not the least bit interested in anything Torrance had to offer. Amused? Yes. Interested? No. He wasn't her thing.

At that moment, Torrance's watch partner, Arturo, walked by. Arturo grabbed Torrance's towel from behind and ripped it down to the floor, never breaking stride, leaving Torrance standing there flexing his muscles, naked, in front of Cynthia.

I imagine that Torrance was feeling very embarrassed by this situation, even more so when Cynthia said to Torrance, while never even leaning forward in her chair or cracking a smile, "Don't worry, Torrance. It'll grow!"

The story of this epic put-down reached me five decks above from where it happened in less than four minutes. I understood that in matters like this I was always the last to know. I'm sure it got around the whole vessel at light speed.

That evening at dinner, everybody was retelling the story, whether they had seen it or not. Wherever you looked, there was a person telling another person, "Don't worry, Torrance. It'll grow!" and then laughing uproariously.

We were all together on that ship for another two months. Torrance turned out to be a good sport, because he heard that multiple times every day and never lost his temper or his mind. Cynthia, on the other hand, while always well considered, achieved legendary and folklorish status with that singular epic retort.

Shortly, we arrived in Ulsan, South Korea, at Hyundai Mipo Shipyard. We were staying in a hotel for a few weeks and soaking up Korean culture. There wasn't much English being spoken, but we made out okay. It's amazing what a useful tool pantomime is!

There was an entertainment district up the hill where all the foreign sailors spent their evenings and their money in the "stand-bars" and brothels, goofing around and hanging out with the working girls. Working girls and merchant sailors have a special relationship. They always have. It's far more than the obvious transactional one that's well understood. I've seen many good friendships develop there. I think it has to do with social position of the professions. Both are on the fringe; both are looked down on by polite society, even to the point of being outcasts. These outcast groups are always looking for easy relationships to take the edge off the inherent loneliness. Both sell something dear to them to make a living, the obvious with the girls, and time, and thus life, for the sailors. You actually do sell your life when you go to sea.

Let me continue with the situation in the bars of Ulsan. They are called stand-bars because they are so small that you often have no place to sit. They are filled with things that your mother threw out from the living room that she furnished in 1962. It's very strange, but you get used to it. It's like a time warp.

Our contingent frequented the Florida Bar. For the record, there are at least a half-dozen Florida Bars in every port city in the world. Peculiarly, they seem all the same too. It's like an episode of *The Twilight Zone.* You almost expect Rod Serling to be lighting a cigarette, leaning on a building on the corner as the camera, black and white of course, zooms out and up.

We learned from the girls there that the big news was that a new brothel was going to be opened around the corner the next evening. The name escapes me, probably some large American city though, like Detroit Bar, San Francisco Bar, Dallas Bar, or maybe even the ubiquitous Zanzibar. We were invited to attend the opening festivities the next night. They were having music, appetizers, and some free beer, and the party was promised to go well into the night. Who could turn down an invitation like that? I wouldn't miss that for the world. Invited to an opening-night party of a brothel in Ulsan, South Korea? Sign us up. In fact, any merchant seaman who misses that opportunity has to turn in his man card on the spot.

So we all squeezed into this small room the next night. We were surprised to see that all the girls were wearing traditional Korean formal garb, gorgeous pastel-colored robes all the way to the floor with layer upon layer of wide cloth belts and a bustle-type construction in the back. Black hair was all done up in combs, along with tons of makeup. They all looked great. Darn near legit!

They must have been getting ready all day long, but it seemed out of place considering what kind of place it was. It was a fun party. Everybody was buying drinks for everybody else, and people were talking and actually behaving. Will wonders never cease?

I remember being especially proud of my bunch. I was sitting behind a table with a beer in front of me, and just on my left side was young Torrance. He was having the most earnest conversation with this nice young lady. I remember hoping she was eighteen but suspecting she might be shy of that by a year or two. It's the New England Puritan in me.

I heard him say, "So with North Korea and South Korea so close to one another, the two countries must be very good friends?"

The young woman he was talking to/romancing made a face like she had just drunk spoiled milk. She looked at him quizzically, as if he'd just stepped off a rocket ship from another planet. She opened her right hand and popped him right in the middle of his forehead with the palm of her open hand. Boink!

She asked, "Torrance, where you been?" She meant that earnestly and with all her heart. I could tell because of the puzzled look she had on her face.

It was another failure of the American primary education to teach social studies and history, and another Torrance moment. Days ran into weeks before the rest of his shipmates stopped trying to *boink* his forehead and asking in a heavy Korean accent, "Torrance, where you been?"

Ulsan got to be a very comfortable and although not the least bit Western, a nice second home ashore. My second mate, Charly, an older, single guy from California, wasted no time in making a semipermanent attachment (actually, it was more of an arrangement than an attachment) to one of the girls. Get that distinction? She was the mama-san in town, actually. She was the head woman who oversaw the goings-on between the sailors and the girls. She was the final arbiter on what went on, what was and was not allowed, what happened between whom, and how people were treated, talked to, and paid.

She was a good bit older than the other girls, had more

experience, and commanded this position of respect very well. Charly told me about this experience with her.

One day she and Charly were walking through the street market like a couple of old married people (according to him), and she stopped at a vendor's stall, one selling the staples like food products, fruits and vegetables, fish, and spices. She reached into a bushel basket, pulled out what looked to be a large, long nut, according to Charly, and put it up to his mouth. He opened his mouth, and she popped it in. He told us that it was crunchy but not bad.

"What is it?" he asked her.

"Bug eat tree. You eat bug." She replied with a wry smile.

Mama-san and I became casual friends. It was part of our jobs. She knew that when I was carrying a briefcase, I was carrying money. That meant the crew was getting paid. And that meant she and her girls were getting paid. She knew her pay days. And I knew, from this roundabout source, what was going on with my crew and how that would affect relationships among the men. It allowed me to stay ahead of any problems. It was convenient.

I wonder where all these people are now, thirty years later. On occasion, I miss them, but certainly never in December when I see the weather coming across the top of the world, through the Bering Sea and into the Gulf of Alaska.

CHAPTER 9

Laguna De Chiriqui Grande, Panama, mid 1980's

How many volumes of scholarly writing have been produced on the topics of space, astronomy and quantum physics? You have to make a guesstimate that several large libraries full might be a sizeable underestimate.

Space, there is a descriptive title if ever there is one. Space is a place so vast that distances are not measured in distance but in light-years, the distance covered by light in one year. In fact, the sun, which is ninety-three million miles from earth, is only nine minutes in light travel away, a mere 0.000017 of a light-year away. If the sun were extinguished right now, we wouldn't know it for nine minutes.

Some of our neighboring galaxies are thousands of light-years away. And when we look at distant stars, we know that the light being seen here on earth at that moment left those stars perhaps even before the earth was formed. If we discern the goings-on on that planet by looking at that light, we would be looking back in time. We are actually viewing the past in real time. It boggles the human mind.

Space is vast amounts of vacuum, filled only with scattered elemental rocks so far as we know at this time. It's a place so large that there is no understanding of where it ends. And if it ends with a wall, for sake of argument, what is on the other side of the wall? And then how far does that go until the next wall? And what is beyond that second wall? And on and on it goes.

The enormity of the challenge of understanding this question is so daunting that we come right back to teaching spherical trigonometry to the dog. It's not going to happen. There are simply too few available neurons in the human brain. Some science-fiction writers have opined that when we get to the end of space, we will find that everything we just traversed is simply the makeup of one small atom of matter that may be one of millions that make up a single cosmic skin cell of a flea that resides on the hindquarters of a stray dog in a second-rated city on a prehistoric planet.

And what is beyond that dog and his existence? It's really too much and is obviously the textbook example of the concept of infinity. For if we can come to an understanding, comprehend an idea fully, or a concept completely, then infinity is not involved. Only when the brain can't stop racing toward an impossible understanding that is never reached can we talk about the infinite. That concept is not difficult, but the completion of that concept into a concrete example is impossible.

And light itself, how much do we know about light? We know the speed of light. We know it is a spectral form of energy. We know gravity can bend light. We know what photons are. We have a rudimentary understanding of the different forms of light, both visible and nonvisible kinds, and we don't know all that much more. If the planet and our civilizations on it survive for thousands of years more, which is at best I'm feeling a fifty-fifty proposition, we may know much more than we know more than we do now.

How much more? Ten times more? One hundred times more? One thousand times more? Which order of magnitude will be the closest? It is arguable that in regards to the study of light, we know very little at this point in human history … very little indeed.

When Albert Einstein took his walks around the campus of Princeton University, it is very likely that this was among the questions he was pondering. And once again, we can point out that the current study of light technology is, for the most part, being funded by governments. For what purpose? Weapons technology. There seems to be that common thread here again. That thread is that new technology is always used in the attempt to secure a military advantage over the enemy. I'll have more on that later.

As an aside, if it makes any of us mortals feel any better about our own inferior positions alongside the strength of Mr. Einstein's intellect, I offer this: It is said that Einstein used to take a small sailing pram out on a pond near where he lived. When his students and colleagues couldn't find him, he was more than once found out on the pond, in that sailing pram, unable to negotiate his way back upwind. It's Sailing 101. Albert Einstein undeniably was a monumental thinker but evidently a very poor sailor. It's interesting. How does that happen? It's something else we do not know.

Einstein was fully engaged with the speed of light. What do we know about that? For instance, why can't the speed of light be surpassed? Does it have something to do with Einstein's theory that if someone were to travel at speeds approaching the speed of light that time would slow down? Time would slow down! Is that not an astounding assertion? Does it not follow that time could go backward? What does that mean? And what does that look like? If the civilization survives and if the understanding of these questions is gained, would that not be the most important discovery in history? History of what? Humans? That seems such a puny standard.

Don't forget that it is entirely possible that all humans are is flea dirt on the hindquarters of an intergalactic stray dog. It's not much. So that is why Einstein called it relativity. These things are only important in the sense of how and from where you are looking at them and how they relate. Smart people, with Einstein-like intellects, have always maintained that you don't want to bet against him. His theories have been proven correct, one by one, as science has developed the means to prove them. Here's a fundamental rule: Don't bet against Einstein.

What's the difference between a futurist and a science-fiction writer? I think there is a lot in common there. These are people who dare to dream about the progress of things through time. They cannot know what the future holds, but looking at history and then current trends, they extrapolate and hypothesize. How do you get a job like that?

When you are seventeen and it's time to go to college, do you tell your parents, "I want to be a futurist"? In our specialized society, I suppose that's laudable.

But think about the futurists. What did Buckminster Fuller do? He posited that people would live in geodesic domes. Way back in the 1960s, the dark ages, geodesic domes were all the rage. I don't see a lot of geodesic domes being built. The futurists have always said that personal flying vehicles are just around the corner. I would guess that's a damn long block they are talking about. The two-wheel Dean Kamen gizmo isn't selling gangbusters, and it's fairly cheap compared to a flying personal vehicle and only moves in two dimensions. Add that third dimension, and society would have to build more hospitals and graveyards to deal with the carnage.

Predicting the future is like predicting the stock market. It can't be done. So what if there's a long-term trend up. It means nothing to the traders when tomorrow's trading opens. There's too many variables. So it's not a useful exercise to look at the trends to try to predict the future. Every day is a new day.

To me this seems like a further case for noknowlogy. The more we know, the less we know. And movement into the future is measured in baby steps. I would not encourage any of my kids to major in futurism, and that's making the wild assumption that there is a future!

Only a few hundred years ago, the cure for a fever was bloodletting. The sicker the patient became, the more blood was let. We know how that generally worked out. In fact, there was so little knowledge of anatomy, biology, chemistry, and pharmacopeia that there were almost no treatments or therapies for any conditions. The human life span was short because of environmental factors and accidents. There were few of the age-related diseases we see now presenting themselves back then. Few people lived long enough to develop dementia, for instance. As a result, the field of medicine was sparsely populated. There were few doctors because there were few patients and there was nothing a doctor could do for a patient anyway.

Communicable diseases were not widely understood. Battlefield wounds were treated with crosscut saws. There was no such thing as anesthesia until William Morton discovered the properties of ether. As closely in time as 1918, flu pandemics caused widespread depopulation. My paternal grandmother, Jenny Rabinowitz, lost her younger sister to that 1918 flu. In the early twentieth century, Harvard University Medical School was teaching its students holistic medicine and natural pharmacology, which proves that what goes around comes around.

So today, we have arguably come a long way. We have soldiers surviving what would have been fatal wounds only a few years ago. We have artificial hearts and heart transplants prolonging lives of patients who would have died without them. We have pediatric heart surgeons operating on their patients in vitro. Can you imagine, operating on a tiny patient's heart before the infant is born? Who thinks of these things, let alone accomplishes them?

In the last hundred years, many deadly diseases have been reduced to footnotes in history, like influenza, whooping cough, rubella, polio, and measles. Vaccinations are nearly a miracle. There is a long list. Sulfa drugs gave way to penicillin, which in turn was replaced with an endless string of antibiotics. Each of which opens up a slew of questions regarding their usage and public health. Deaths from bacterial infection have plummeted as result. We have orthopedic surgery and reconstructions whose only previous treatment was amputation. We have transplanted almost all of the major organs in the human body. We grow skin cells in Petri dishes for burn patients. We have learned to treat cancers in an ever more effective way, resulting in improved outcomes and longer life spans. There is promising research going on right now with researchers hot on the trail of cures for other disease and conditions such as ALS, cystic fibrosis, autism, multiple sclerosis, Parkinson's, traumatic brain injury, and a host of others. Still we must agree that as much as we have discovered and know, there is much more to be learned than what we already know. No reasonable person could disagree.

I previously mentioned that medical treatment on a ship has always been a dubious prospect at best. There is no requirement for a doctor on any merchant vessel of the world that do not carry more than 12 passengers. Traditionally this chore has always fallen to the ship's master. He alone is responsible for the health, safety, and welfare of the crew, so that makes sense. As long as people have been going to sea on ships, there have been deaths at sea because of both the nature of the work and the lack of top-quality medical care. Often accidents are the cause of injuries requiring this substandard medical care. Many times it's just illnesses that can cause problems up to and including death. If your exposure to the seagoing life lasts long enough, you will be touched directly or indirectly by this circumstance.

I was master on a medium-size tankship back in the 1980s. We were running between Laguna de Chiriqui Grande on the Caribbean side and north of the Panama Canal and the Mississippi River. We were hauling crude oil to the local refineries that had been brought down from Alaska and offloaded on the Pacific side of the Trans Panama Pipeline. It was pumped across Panama to a storage facility at Chiriqui Grande, where it was reloaded on ships that took it to a variety of Gulf Coast refineries, where it was refined into products for the American market, such as gasoline, diesel oil, jet fuel, heating oil, and any other number of oil-based solvents and lubes. These ships were all much too large to transit the canal while loaded. That's why we took the cargo off the ship on the Pacific side and reloaded it on the Caribbean side.

We were in the Laguna, awaiting a loading buoy to open up. It was easy living, swinging gently at the end of a seventy five fathom chain with the port anchor, all ten tons of cast steel holding us firmly in position. There's an old rule of thumb that when your anchoring in the Northern Hemisphere, you should use the port anchor. Southern Hemisphere favors the starboard anchor. Professional mariners have spent a lot of time discussing that rule, its origin, its reasons, and its folklore. Perhaps it's another chapter in another book.

I had the deck gang rig out a high-velocity fog applicator, a piece of required firefighting gear connected to a fire hose, and this gentle spray was running twenty-four hours for any of the crew who wanted to put on a bathing suit and get wet. It was at least 90 degrees Fahrenheit, so there were plenty of takers. Swimming from the ship was possible but not a good idea. The water was so clear you could see the large nurse and bull sharks that swam slowly around the ship with attached remoras hitching a ride. The natives were crossing our path ahead and behind us in dugout canoes made from mahogany logs and powered with small outboard motors of various ages and states of repair. There were cloudless skies except for when there was the daily one-hour tropical downpour.

There was no wind. There were beautiful sunsets and sunrises. There were brilliant displays of the night sky because of lack of man-made ambient light pollution. I used to think how I could stand on the wing of that very same bridge at times like this, and it was such a low blood pressure moment. At other times, for different reasons, in various places and circumstances, standing on the very same spot on the wing of the bridge, it could be so much different, a very high blood pressure moment.

Jorge DeSanto was one of my best sailors. He was an immigrant from the Azores. He spoke Portuguese as a first language and lived in the large Azorian community in Rhode Island. He was a good guy, as well as gentle, competent, and funny as hell. He had the driest sense of humor around. He used to do his versions of the skits showing on *Saturday Night Live*, which kept everyone in stitches. Occasionally the chef on the ship would let him whip up a Bacalao for the crew. It's impossible to duplicate, and I've tried many a time. Man, that fellow could cook.

We were at anchor in Laguna De Chiriqui Grande when Jorge had his stroke. As luck would have it, this was to be Jorge's last trip since he was retiring. The chef had made him a retirement cake that was put away for just the next day at sea, when we were going to have a BBQ and retirement party for Jorge, as soon as we departed Panama.

Luckily, I thought, *this is not the worst stroke I've seen*. Jorge was having some trouble with his face and speaking. He could walk. I instantly knew I had to get him off the vessel, onto a plane, and up to Miami, the closest US port to Panama with suitable hospitals and doctors, as soon as I could without delay.

I called my local agent on the VHF radio and told him to get over here and what I wanted him to do. I put Jorge on a launch and took him to the hospital in Chiriqui Grande to await a ride to Panama City, where he could fly out. The hospital at Chiriqu Grande was a log and thatched hut with no windows and no equipment. It was on the main street, which wasn't a street at all. It was a four-foot-wide concrete sidewalk. Along the sides of the sidewalk were lots of extension cords and three-quarter-inch PVC pipes to supply the villagers with water and minimal power. There aren't a lot of places on earth that are more primitive, and I'm one to know.

Jorge and I took a seat in the hospital, where I noticed an old, cracked, and rusty porcelain basin full of water filled with floating hypodermic needles. None of which made me feel better.

When the agent arrived, I told him he was driving Jorge immediately over the mountains and not dare stop till he got to the international airport in Panama City and had Jorge on a plane to Miami. I put Jorge in the 4WD SUV and shook his hand. He was out of there, so I thought.

Back on the ship, I made a satellite call to headquarters in Houston and informed fleet operation what had happened and what I had arranged. I asked them to keep me posted. I then got hold of the US Council at the embassy in Panama City and alerted the *chargé d'affaires* to our U.S. citizen who was being medically repatriated. I gave them the details so they could assist. It's their job. That's why they are there.

Over the next forty-eight hours, we got very busy. There's a lot of federal paperwork repatriating a US citizen from a foreign country under these circumstances, and that kept me busy. We put the ship up to the loading buoy. We loaded the vessel and sailed for the US Gulf.

The entrance channel to the Laguna De Chiriqui Grande was over fifty feet deep. The water was so clear you could see the bottom, a very unusual and wholly unreal phenomena. There I was on a loaded vessel drawing forty-three feet of water and I could see the bottom. It was tremendously unsettling. You think that at any moment you're going to come up hard aground, tear the bottom out, end up on television news shows worldwide, and spend a large portion of the rest of your life in jail and certainly broke. What about the kids? What would happen to my wife and kids? It was crazy town. Transiting that channel never failed to evoke that response. That's another book on the thoughts, dreams, and nightmares that shipmasters have and may follow. I might possibly win a prize for that one if they give out prizes for "nuts."

Once out to sea, I began to make phone calls because I was concerned about how Jorge was making out. Our office stateside told me that Jorge was in a hospital in Panama City. The local doctors had wanted to keep him there. They didn't want him to fly. Two days later, Jorge passed away, still in that damn Panamanian hospital. I was distraught, furious, and disgusted.

I have very few regrets concerning my seagoing days. This is the one at the top of the list. There's nothing else I could have done, but the shipmaster's most sacred duty is to bring all your people home to their families. I was not able to do this. We learn our lessons, often the hard way. Sometimes with others paying the price. But we have to live and continue on. It's odd how life sometimes works. I know this much: I've thought about Jorge and his family often these last thirty or so years and will undoubtedly continue to do so. It goes with the job I used to do. It's collateral damage.

I recall that we were out to sea, rounding the western tip of Jamaica, heading northwest toward the US Gulf Coast, when we heard the news of Jorge's passing. We had a simple prayer service, read a passage or two from the Bible, and prayed together for his soul and strength for his family. Tears flowed freely. Afterward we each had a slice of the retirement cake that he never got to see. It tasted bittersweet to me. God has a wicked curveball.

CHAPTER 10

A day at the races, New York, 1973

Just a few short generations ago, a couple of brilliantly eccentric bicycle mechanics and brothers from Ohio flew a heavier-than-air aircraft off the sands of Kitty Hawk, North Carolina. Only fifteen short years after that first flight, pilots on both sides of a world war were completing insane acrobatic maneuvers in an attempt to machine gun, shoot down, and kill their opposite numbers. Only twenty-five years after that and in the midst of another world war, the sides built huge aircraft with multiple engines to fly at tens of thousands of feet for thousands of miles in order to drop tons of explosives on both the enemy and their civilian populations. A single raid over Tokyo killed eighty thousand people in one night. The efficiency in this horrific bloodletting was as astounding as it was awful.

The jet engine appeared, and the world became smaller. Huge

airliners flying higher and faster than ever before transported millions of people to far-flung destinations all around the globe. Journeys that took months were—and are—completed in hours. And the safety record accomplishing that can't be equaled. You stand a much greater chance being injured walking down the street than flying in a large commercial airliner. And thanks to WWII weapons programs, we have walked on the moon. The Apollo program is a direct descendant of Werner von Braun's VII rocket program of that war.

We are only 115 years into this era of flight. Look at what has been accomplished. But is this the zenith of where we are taking this field? What will occur in the next hundred years? Is there any reason to believe this will stop? Already daredevils are putting on synthetic fabric suits, strapping miniature jet engines to their backs, and taking flight! What could be next? What do we not know about the future of aeronautics? I suspect there is much not yet known.

All these tech companies producing tech devices is a new phenomenon. The rate is accelerating at which new tech devices are superseding old ones. Or is it? It wasn't too long ago on the timeline of progress when scientists, engineers, mathematicians, and astronomers brought their fields together to produce celestial navigation a much older kind of technology. For hundreds of years, this miraculous and complicated technical field was a high-tech field unto itself.

These days you can navigate a merchant vessel with an electronic instrument that is no bigger than a pack of cigarettes. What people don't realize is that the military controls the systems that allow this accuracy and convenience. If there is ever an emergency or attack on the nation or national interest, one switch and seven seconds later there is no so such thing as electronic navigation. It's a national security thing. An adversary's cruise missile loaded with a conventional or other type of warhead could easily follow our own electronic navigation right into the most sensitive of targets. The generals simply cannot have that.

As a populace, we can't allow it either. As a result, all these global satellite systems are able to be secured in just moments. Those navigational satellites that belong to our adversaries will mostly be taken out by satellite-killing technology almost immediately at the onset of hostilities. There's no reason for anyone to think the enemy isn't prepared to do the same to ours. It makes sense.

The point is that at any moment, all these wonderful electronic navigational devices can go dark and stay that way for who knows how long. We will be right back to the last century—charts, dividers, triangles, and taffrail logs. Sextants were the main (and most high-tech) tool of the trade for ship's deck officers in those days and for the previous several centuries.

Sextants measure the angle of heavenly bodies to the horizon. (No, not that kind of heavenly body!) Knowing that angle and applying trigonometric functions and time to that number, a procedure known as reducing, when plotted on a chart or plotting sheet, will provide a line of position. Two or more lines of position that intersect will provide a position, a representation on a chart where the ship is on the surface of the globe. It is essential for safely delivering cargo and not running the vessel aground. The entire enterprise, taken as a whole, is called celestial navigation. And it has been largely replaced by the aforementioned gizmos, gadgets, and transistors. That is another philosophical argument we may or may not come back to. Perhaps that's later.

My good friend and previously introduced pal and mentor, Steven Choo, owned the most beautiful Plath sextant anybody ever saw. It had been lovingly manufactured in West Germany and certified by Mr. Charles Plath himself to be totally accurate. Steven carried it with him everyplace he went in a polished mahogany box with brass fittings. Anyone who knew what Steven had in the box he carried lusted after it.

As a cadet, the Merchant Marine Academy had loaned me a sextant that was made of scrap razor blades and beer cans and had been dropped, punted, and otherwise abused by so many previous cadets since it had been manufactured by a well-known sewing machine company during WWII that its usability was more suited as a small boat anchor than a navigational instrument.

One day when we were out to sea and on watch, Steven was producing perfect sunlines with his Plath on that morning 8:00 to 12:00 watch. I asked him where and when he procured the magnificent instrument. He told me a story that I will repeat for you now.

"So I'm staying at the doghouse, the dormitory over the union hall next to the Irish Bar down in the Battery. I'm nearly out of money, but I've got a really old union card [a killer card, as they are known], so I throw in my card for a third mate's job that has just come up on the board, on an old C-3 like this one, also to West Africa. I hate West Africa, but I had the oldest card and needed a job, so I get a physical exam from the doctor right there in the bar. You should have seen the look on the face of guy who walked in the bar's front door as the doctor told me to turn my head and cough, standing right there at the bar, drink in hand, and pants pulled down around knees. I don't think that drunken doctor even washed his hands before turning back to his drink! I was headed over by the subway to Twenty-Third Street in Brooklyn to join the ship. But before I go, I have a few more shots of whiskey with the guys from the Union Hall because … well … just because. So I get to Isthmian Terminal in Brooklyn and get up the gangway, seabag in one hand and my old sextant in other, on this rust bucket C-3 named the *Steel Vendor* built in 1943 and looking every day of it. But a job's a job. [He pronounced it 'yob's a yob.'] I climb up the ladders and go see the old man to sign on. The shipping commissioner was there too, so I sign on. How I 'spose to know that the old man was teetotaler, and I guess he took offense to my breath and the whiskey and all. So I find my room and start unpacking my things when, only a minute later, the old man is standing in my doorway looking mad and unhappy. He points at me and says, 'Mr. Choo, you fired! Pack your bags! When you get back to hall, you tell them … no drunks on my ship!'

"So fifteen minutes later, I'm standing on the sidewalk outside the terminal at 23rd Street in Brooklyn. Fired, unemployed, nearly broke, and worst … sobering up. *What to do, Steven?* I think. So I get back on the subway and head out to the horse track on Long Island. I'm down to my last twenty bucks. Right there in front of me on the racing form, fourth race, is the number-three horse named Pack Your Bags."

He jammed his right index finger into his left palm as if it were the racing form. He was pointing out the entry.

To this day, I remember Steven Choo looking me in the eye with his rheumy eyes, a dark spot in the white field in the left one and the other not quite looking straight at me. He was very proud as he told me this story. He puffed out his chest, picked up his chin, and smiled with satisfaction as he continued, "Fourth race, number-three horse named Pack Your Bags! Thirty-to-one odds! Dat my horse!"

His voice was rising an octave still, five years after the event, as he poked himself on his breastbone with an arthritic finger, grinning ear to ear, almost imperceptibly nodding his head in heartfelt congratulations to himself.

Pack Your Bags came in for Steven that afternoon at Aqueduct. He collected his $600 winnings, bought the Plath sextant in a nautical shop down near the battery for $400 in 1969 dollars, a princely sum, and had enough left over to catch another ship the next week. I've heard things work out the way they are supposed to. It's so true.

So Steven had his horse come in at Aqueduct. These things happen. It's a branch of mathematics called probabilities. The usefulness of that bit of knowledge makes me think that the existence of God may well be a matter of probabilities as well. What are we looking at though? A billion-to-one for the existence? Or a billion-to-one against? Or would you prefer the argument for a fifty-fifty proposition? Making the argument that God either exists or He or She doesn't exist (or is even gendered) should produce that fifty-fifty proposition. You will remember that the brilliant American writer Samuel Clemens wrote that there are liars, damn liars, and statisticians. But still there is the usefulness of the mathematics.

A friend I respect recently bought a ticket in a huge lottery worth more than a billion dollars. I asked him why he didn't double his odds of winning the enormous prize by buying two lottery tickets.

He replied, "No need for that. If God wants you to win, all you need is one ticket, but you have to buy at least one ticket because if you don't do that, even God can't help you!"

The logic seems inescapable. There is a lot to be said about probabilities and God. We will return there later.

CHAPTER 11

Meeting Chief Engineer Nunzio Striglio Bayonne, N.J. 1976

Human beings have been in search of shelter since they evolved from having a coat of fur, if you are a follower of Darwin on the HMS *Beagle.* Dogs need little shelter. They have a complicated system of layers of fur that keep them cool in the summer and warm in the winter. Some animals have thick layers of fur, bears, for example, that keep them dry. Birds have a complicated system of feathering that performs much the same function. It is elegant in design, highly decorative for attracting mates, and camouflaging against predators while also being highly functional in terms of protecting the animal from the elements and adding little weight to a living machine that flies! The fact there are commonly so many birds in everyday life makes it no less astounding.

Human beings have no such protection. They build their shelters wherever they go. It is an imperative for their survival. So in the early years, humans were in search of caves, hollows of trees, and outcropping of rock that would provide shelter, however minimal, from weather and predators. Next came lean-tos' made out of tree limbs, branches, and palm fronds. When textiles were introduced, it wasn't long before humans used textiles to shield themselves from the sun and the other elements.

Tents became popular and still are for an effective, inexpensive, and portable shelter. Tents provide their users some degree of protection from the sun, cold, snow, and rain. They can be carried easily from site to site.

Next came blocks of stone and then boards sawn from felled trees. Cabins were pegged together with branches pounded through holes in logs made by iron augers. Roofs were made of sod or palm fronds.

As technology developed and new materials became available, architecture developed as both an art and a science. So it is today. Styles of architecture changed frequently, falling out of favor and being rethought in many of the revivals: modernism, minimalism, classical, neoclassical, Elizabethan, or Victorian. The styles come and go and come back again.

Every new material allowed the artists and engineers to build new styles of structures. When hydraulics were introduced, Gustave Eiffel was able to employ them in a way that made elevators possible and the building of the Eiffel Tower in Paris a practical endeavor.

Shortly after and because of Mr. Otis's elevator, developers and engineers in New York City were able to build that city's first skyscraper. The building is still in use and doing as well physically as any other of New York's skyscrapers. Structural glass led to the natural development of the curtain wall where sheets of glass were hung to form the skin of a building built entirely of steel. The rest is history.

Frank Lloyd Wright pioneered the use of cantilevered reinforced concrete deck structures. The resultant horizontal lines of those structures developed into the Prairie style that he became famous for. Time has not been kind to some of those cantilevered structures, and as decades have passed, many have needed substantial structural repair. Gravity is relentless, particularly over time.

Man has built notable and fantastic dwellings, workplaces, monuments, and civil projects. The history has been that as new materials are developed, engineers and architects utilize them to build these projects. It is done in the furtherance of the art and science and in the search for less cost and more utility.

Do we really know what is next? In a thousand or more years, what will our architecture look like? Will there be a new set of problems, not yet even realized, that dictates the parameters of these projects? What is it that we do not know about this that will certainly affect this endeavor? We can be certain that we have not reached the end of the line in this field.

People don't like getting their feet wet, like cats, I guess. If there is a stream, you can bet that someone will pull a felled tree across it so they can walk across it without slipping on a rock or getting their feet wet. As the art of bridge building turned into the science of civil engineering, the structures have gotten bigger, more impressive, and more useful. It's the same with dams, dikes, levees, sewer systems, potable water systems, and electrical grids. Progress is progressing progressively. Can we take a position that civil engineering has reached its zenith?

I would not support that supposition. I think that although we have a logical and useful basis in that field, there is absolutely no telling what the future may bring. Maybe someday we will be able to take an elevator all the way to outer space on a miles-high tower. Maybe we can take a ride through a tunnel in the center of the earth? Who can know? Noknowlogy. It's more of what we do not know

Artificial intelligence, is that an oxymoron? So the computer, only a hundred years old and invented in England by a bunch of smart mathematicians to break codes (here's that wartime/weaponized thing again) is going to replicate human intellect. I will not bet against that proposition, as far a stretch as it seems.

What is intelligence? It's an arrangement of electrical patterns controlling thought, behavior, and, most astoundingly, creativity from the human brain to the rest of the organism. It's a biologically based process that finds these electrical signals created, patterned, and stored in a chemical bath, like a bad Hollywood-grade B horror movie. If that's not astounding enough, perhaps miraculous, we call the idiosyncratic parts of this learning personality. Psychology, psychiatry, brain science, and neurology, field after field, is being explored by really smart, educated folks.

Every day on this planet, ten million new brains join the world. Who did that? Or what did that? Or who is doing that, for those not theologically inclined? I assert all these fields of immense learning are at a point today in 2019 that medicine was at when the only treatment was bloodletting and the barber performed it.

Think about that. It's noknowlogy, and I assert that we don't know squat about the brain. Or if you argue that we know considerably more than squat about the brain, I will counter that the percentage of what we know now to what we will find out in the next two hundred years is less than 5 percent. And I think that is being generous.

I have no doubt that Silicon Valley whiz kids will use patterns of ones and zeroes to replicate what may pass for artificial intelligence. That will be little more than a parlor trick. I don't think I'll be around when a computer paints a series of paintings like Van Gogh did at Arles as his life spiraled out of control and into madness. Maybe there will be a "crazy" button on the painting computer to replicate that too. The possibilities are endless. We just don't know what is to follow.

Communications is a vital and necessary part of the human condition. Our ability to speak and communicate, more than any other trait, sets us apart from the rest of the animals we share the planet with. Ancient languages flourished and died with the societies that used them. Through all this, the need to communicate has never changed. Humans communicate. As technology is developed, the number of ways that we communicate has increased. We have conquered distance and time in our communications.

First there was just speech. Humans would talk to each other. They also painted in caves in order to make permanent records of their activities, which would communicate those activities to others in the future. When languages were established, systems of writing were developed. People could write down what was spoken, and others, fluent in the written word, could read exactly what was being communicated. The written word also allowed conversations and thought to be maintained for posterity, first on stone and then vellum, parchment, and now paper. Modern technology has made the "paperless" promise where what was formerly physically recorded on paper would be stored and displayed on digital media instead. We have come a long way from reel-to-reel tape recorders. The promise has yet to be fulfilled, but the horizon to that goal is ever closer. Just consider the Apple Store.

Communications has become a huge field, and there is much to be said about it and its impact on the planet, in particular the human condition. We went from talking to yelling, smoke signals, megaphones, signal flags, flashing lights, telegraph, telephone, pager, email, text, fiber optics and finally to who knows what's next.

We are attempting to communicate far out in the galaxy. Communication is one of the things we do best. And when we are not at our best communicating, often trouble results.

In the mid-1970s, I joined my first ship as a third mate. An old baby supertanker, it was called back then, barely twenty-eight thousand tons. It is small by today's standards but carried a crew of over forty men. It was sailing coastwise carrying clean (refined) products from Gulf Coast refineries to Northeastern US metropolitan areas not yet served by pipeline.

I climbed up the gangway to the earsplitting whine of steam turbine cargo pumps that were moving the cargo ashore at one of the many New Jersey piers where we were to discharge. This old ship, built in 1953, was beaten but well maintained and a big earner for both its crew and ownership.

I walked forward toward the forward deck house where I knew I would find the captain. I needed to "sign on," which would make me official. I would then find the mate I was scheduled to relieve so he could go home on paid leave, having been aboard for more than three months.

I stepped over the threshold of an old mahogany door replete with a brass porthole and tarnished brass hardware, thinking that they didn't build them like this anymore. Inside there were lots of coats of paint. She was clean and smelled of disinfectant. She was lit with bare incandescent light bulbs in a short-skirted brass ceiling fixture. She might have been worn, but she was cared for. Rounding a corner, I bumped into a small Filipino-looking man who was pushing a mop bucket on wheels with a mop. He smiled broadly, and we said hello. He was the bedroom steward, and his job was to clean up, make beds, and help out wherever needed.

As I walked by an open door on the way to the stairwell to the master's suite, I looked inside what turned out to be a laundry room. Pipes and wires on the overhead were painted over. Metal grates in a buff color. Angle iron stiffeners hung on steel walls. There was more of the same lighting. I saw a wringer-style washing machine (more on that later) and an electric clothes dryer. A hinged ironing board was affixed to the wall. Standing there was a man with one hand on the top of the wringer, facing the wall. He was just standing there naked as the day he was born!

The machine splashed back and forth, a murky gray-green water gurgling with a few iridescent soap bubbles on top. He turned his head and looked at me while I tried to say hello in an appropriate way to a naked man doing his laundry in a public laundry room. He nodded. I swallowed, nodded, and scurried off to the stairs, making good speed.

I found the master's office, and old Captain Jones was sitting at his desk. I saw a shock of uncombed gray hair. His sleeveless T-shirt stretched over many years of good eating on the ships. We introduced ourselves and shook hands. We made a little small talk about my hometown, which he picked up from my Merchant Mariner's "Z" card. I signed the coastwise articles and a USCG discharge for when my time on the vessel was over.

On my way out to find the fellow I was relieving, I turned and asked the old man, "What's the deal with the naked guy, Captain?"

He laughed and explained, "That's Nunzio Striglio, the chief engineer. In the war he was torpedoed several times. He lives here in Bayonne, and when his paid leave is over, he walks to the ship in his green jumpsuit. That's it. Green jumpsuit, pair of underwear, socks, shoes, a toothbrush, and a razor in his pocket. Folds up his license in his pocket and hangs it up as soon as he gets aboard. He likes to travel light so he doesn't lose anything if he's ever torpedoed again."

I said, "No vessel has been torpedoed in over thirty years."

(A few years later, a British attack submarine in the Falklands War put a torpedo into the Argentine cruiser *General Belgrano*, rolling her over and killing hundreds and hundreds. It's still a lethal technology.)

"Doesn't matter. That's Nunzio," the captain said. "Every day at four o'clock he comes out of the engine room and heads for the laundry, strips down, and washes his clothes, standing there as naked as a jaybird. We kid him that he better be careful where he stands in relation to that wringer-style washing machine, if you get my drift."

We both laughed.

The captain continued, "He takes a shower in his room across the hall, dries off, goes back to the laundry room naked, gets dressed, and comes to dinner. Been doing that every day for more years than I can remember."

That's the story of Nunzio Striglio, chief engineer. Regarding that wringer washing machine, these ships all roll (sway back and forth, side to side) heavily at sea. If an automatic washer were installed every time the ship rolled, the unbalanced load sensor would shut it off. On the old-style wringer machines, it just continues to run. That's why even modern vessels are equipped with wringer washers. But you have to be careful. Certainly you don't want to get anything caught in the wringer!

CHAPTER 12

Matching wits with a master

By now, the reader will have a fairly broad, certainly not in-depth, overview of a few of the subjects and fields of study in which we know an impressive amount of information, however that is measured. I have been trying for many chapters to impress that the sum of that vast knowledge is miniscule in comparison to that which remains undiscovered or just beyond our reach because of developmental deficiencies in the human brain in this twenty-first century.

To my way of thinking, this is obvious. To deny it means we are done learning new things. The cures to diseases will not be discovered. That which lies beyond the galaxies will not be understood now or in the future. The tallest building has already been built. The deepest crevice of underwater trenches has already been explored. That's saying not a single new discovery in computing will be unveiled. That does seem among the absurd if the past and present have any ability whatsoever to predict the future. If I have not made that point clearly enough or the reader thinks that this a patently false premise or just malicious claptrap, the book ends here. For that reader, there is no point continuing. Perhaps they can get their purchase price back to buy a box of chocolates, Kleenex, or something similarly useful to them.

To the rest, I will lay out a straightforward path to a circuitous assumption. That assumption is that for any of us, this newest of attempts at understanding what we don't know may reaffirm our faith in the existence of God. There, I have said it. It has not been easy to get here or to get that out. I can almost hear books slamming shut nationwide as well as the muttering and head shaking of disaffected readers as they turn out the lights and head for bed. But, if they bear with me, invest a bit more time and open their mind to the possibilities, there may be a fresh outlook ahead.

What else can one ask for? I certainly can't promise eternal life, although we don't really know that either. I just spent chapters on the provable existence of the probably impossible, the unthinkable, and the unknowable. What would make something impossible—provably, absolutely impossible. What makes things impossible? Perhaps it's the lack of the willingness to believe. But it's certainly nothing physical. I can only present what looks like it makes sense. Perhaps it could make sense to you too?

Who said "if man can dream it, he can do it"? That is an interesting proposition. Is it not? I tend to agree with that. Science fiction stretches us out in that direction. Jules Verne's and Captain Nemo's submarine was science fiction, and now submarine technology is well understood and commonplace, if not yet fully developed. Consider the Dick Tracy wrist radio. We have eclipsed that proposition tenfold. And once again, we see that the technology that humans develop finds its early and often primary uses in weapons technology. It seems to me that if someone hasn't already done it, there is a chance to have a new law named in the science of anthropology or psychology. It happens regularly and without fail. And it's looking like a hardwired trait of the human being, especially the male of the species.

Watch any male toddler while his brothers or sisters are

competing on the Saturday morning athletic fields. He will pick up a stick, any stick, and begin to swing it at things. It is a weapon, specifically his. He will not give it up easily. He will be indignant at any attempt to take it away from him. He will cry with frustration and anger when it is taken from him. He will defiantly rebel at any attempt to censure him. That's what little boys do, with few, if any, observable exceptions! You don't need a PhD in psychology to know that. I would say to any person who wants to argue against that observation, "Sorry, you're wrong. You have not been paying attention."

Further examples from the adult male (and to be fair, some females) include:

- Stone Age: axes and arrowheads
- Bronze Age: swords
- medieval physics: siege engines, truncheons, and catapults
- steam power: warships
- combustion engines: tanks and military vehicles
- radio technology: Military communications hardware
- undersea technology: submarines
- flight: fighter and reconnaissance aircraft
- atomic fission and fusion: bombs
- lasers: targeting, range-finding, and beam weapons
- computer technology—gosh, what kind of weapons are computers now being used for—electronic navigation Loran, Gee, Radar, and GPS, which have many obvious military uses

We could call it Ehab's law. Now if you're a pessimistic type, instead of calling it military technology, you could substitute "killing people" and decry the principal point of Ehab's law. Who could argue with that assessment? History is littered with battlefield after battlefield, each full of proof.

The optimist will celebrate it instead and insist that it is great benefit to humankind because it allows societies to defend themselves and to maintain the peace. It allows progress. Peace through strength has been shown to work as well, that is, as long as the right people are in charge of these weapons and the peace.

This is where we get ready to step into the quicksand. How you look at these things then becomes a matter of political philosophy, something, admittedly, I profess to know little about beyond the obvious. Perhaps that is a future field of study and another treatise of some sort, but there is little point in obscuring the waters of noknowlogy with a contentious political battle in this the year 2019.

Yes, politics should be left alone at this time but cannot be. How people organize themselves for the greater good is important in this discussion and cannot legitimately be avoided, particularly when these topics account for a large percentage of all the human misery and deaths on earth, exclusive of natural causes and diseases. It is a consequential topic, no doubt.

Captain Phillip Storm was one of the best captains I ever worked for. I am probably the only one of his ex–chief officers to say that. He really was a pain in the ass, even to me, and I say that with nothing but love in my heart for the man. There never was a smarter man or a more contrary one. Whatever you said, his retort was, "No … you're wrong," loudly, clearly, and in front of whoever was there.

But I saw the good in the man, and there was a lot of it. He was quite overweight, and perched in his high captain's chair in the corner of the bridge, he looked like Jabba the Hutt. He squinted out of one eye constantly. Everything he uttered sounded like a question. He growled when he talked and had some kind of swallowing disorder that made him cough and clear his throat a lot. It didn't help that he was an unrepentant chain-smoker. Marlboros were his poison. He never flicked his ashes off. He would let them grow longer and longer until they fell off naturally and hit him in his considerable belly and thence to the deck.

Conversation with him had a rhythm that included the ash

falling off and dropping on his belly. After a two count, it was down to the deck. He used that sequence as theatrical punctuation when he wanted to make a strong point. The ash would fall to the belly and then deck. In the smallest of ways, it was amazing how he did that. He was a private pilot before he lost his license to health concerns. He was a businessman, a stock picker, and a philanthropist. Fun for him was exploring the Yangtze River on a junk in the days before his wife became ill. There were several buildings named after him on his hometown's state college campus. He had been working hard for more than forty years and had enjoyed the tremendous growth of the multinational company we were working for. He was a far piece past financially comfortable.

One of the sailors asked him one time, "Captain, you've got plenty of dough. Why don't you retire and go home with your wife and have fun?"

His reply was, "When I'm on the ship, I can tell any one of you sons of bitches to go take out the garbage. When I'm home, all I hear is 'Phillip, you take out the garbage right now!' That's why!"

We could talk. For me, there was plenty to learn from a man that bright. He had a wealth of experience. I could ask him all kind of things, and he was more than happy to tell me. More important than the technical was the philosophical and political. He had a lot to say, and I just listened. He was in his sixties; I was in my twenties. What was he going to learn from me? Nothing! So I listened.

We were well up in San Francisco Bay one winter afternoon in the early 1980s. Upon finishing the discharge of cargo, we made ready for sea. That was my job. I was the chief mate at that time. The hours were brutal. If it were an in-port operation, I was in charge, so after several twenty-four-hour days of manual labor, I was beat. We made fast the tugboats, let go the lines fore and aft, and backed off the pier. We headed downstream toward the Pacific Ocean, about a three- or four-hour trip. Then under the Golden Gate Bridge, there was a turn north at the Farallon Islands,

Point Reyes, a few miles to starboard and north, and five days to Alaska making sea speed if weather allowed.

We stowed everything we could and made the vessel ready for sea. At the time, the port anchor was walked out of the hawse pipe, hanging just above the water, in a position ready to be dropped at a moment's notice. It was out in that position because that's the way the captain preferred to have it transiting inland waters, for safety purposes in case we would have to let it go quickly in event of an emergency or propulsion failure. It would have to be pulled into the hawse pipe for stowage in order to go to sea. Leaving it out of the hawse pipe at sea is never an option. It needed to be stowed and secured with heavy chains so it wouldn't be lost at sea or slammed into the ship by waves at sea, possibly damaging the ship.

So I left the main deck, climbed up five decks, and poured a cup of steaming hot coffee on the bridge. I stood next to the captain as we proceeded down the channel, observing the harbor pilot give rudder and engine commands to the helmsman and third mate. It was quiet, and things were winding down. The radars and the gyrocompass were humming reassuringly. The sun was setting behind the hills of Marin County, ahead in the distance.

The radio crackled, and the junior third mate, on the bow, came over the small speaker, "Mate, we are all secured up here except for the anchor. Do you want me to bring it home and secure it now while I have the guys up here, or are you going to get it later?"

I was thinking, *If the third mate gets the anchor now, I can relax after seventy-two straight hours of pounding the deck. If I have to get it later, that means I pass out in my chair now, get up in two or three hours, feeling like hell, trek seven hundred feet in the dark, in a blowing wind, and then bring the anchor home and stow it in the dark on a rolling ship.*

I certainly knew exactly what I wanted him to do, but I could see/feel Old Man Storm squinting at me out of the corner of my eye, ready to pounce. I was certain whatever I said he would have a different answer, for no other reason than that's how he operated. He was a contrarian, foremost and always.

I replied to the mate, "No, Mate, leave it out, please. I'll come up there later and get it."

The radio crackled. "Roger that."

The old man growled, cleared his throat, shook his leonine head, and said firmly, "No. Tell him to stow it now."

I stared straight ahead in the darkening bridge and told the mate, "Change in plans. Go ahead and stow the anchor now, please."

I stood there for a moment, enjoying the only single victory I ever scored over Captain Phillip Storm, however small. I took a very satisfying sip of coffee as I thought about the long sleep I was about to embark on.

What made it just a little better was that I could see him peripherally sitting in his chair, long-ashed cigarette hanging from his lips, staring out of his squinty eye at the side of my head. Electricity was behind his eyes. I'm sure he realized at that moment that he'd been had, bested, just that once, but bested nonetheless!

A year or two later, Captain Storm was on his last trip before retirement. He was cleaning out his desk. He handed me a small brass fertility charm he had picked up from somewhere in Southeast Asia. It was in the shape of a troll. It had a huge erect phallus that was in fact larger than the rest of the troll's body.

He said to me, "Mate, every ship has to have a prick. Now that I'm going, I guess that's going to be you!"

He gave me the little brass statue, and I have it here with me today. Thank you, Captain Storm. My pleasure!

CHAPTER 13

Hooray for me and Fuck you. Greenland, Late 1930's

Let's explore a little bit about organized religion. There's a subject that has born more than its share of scrutiny, particularly of late. I will try not to produce too many words on this subject. The goal is to say enough to make the point. That will be enough. Leading the reader down path after path, with examples, footnotes, and discussions including rebuttals, will obscure the point to be made. That point of contention is: How does organized religion and what we do not know about its central figure, God, relate to faith and the reality, which are both physical and other worldly? Does God exist? Does He or She not? Is there proof? Is there not? Is faith required, or is the proof plain to see? There are lots of questions. Many people who think about these things are satisfied with the answers they have received in the osmosis of the subject while living in religious or partly religious societies. Many are not.

Organized religion—Judaism, Christianity, Buddhism, Islam, and Hinduism—have a lot in common. They have millions of followers, in some cases, billions. They are for the most part all ancient religions and go back thousands of years, although some might opine that thousands of years from a cosmic view of things might hardly qualify as ancient at all. Nonetheless, centuries, as far as people are concerned, is not an insignificant amount of time. The religions all have a faith in God.

What is faith? Faith is the acceptance of conditions that fact cannot prove. Many scholarly and otherwise important volumes have been written on this subject, too many to enumerate how humans reject, accept, or just deal with faith in a very personal matter. Each must make his or her own choice. Regarding the existence of God, faith is a requirement. If one has faith that God exists, that is the same as saying that faith is required because there is no proof. On the other hand, you can have faith in the existence of God without having faith in the deity itself or the power or even importance of the deity. That is an entirely different discussion. There can be a lot of parsing of words in this discussion. The central point is that if it's organized religion, there is a requirement of a certain amount of faith in the precepts and tenets of that religion.

Dogma is the teachings, stories, rituals, regulations, requirements, tradition, writing, and teachings of the religion to the faithful. This is where organized religion gets a bit dicey for some. Take the vestments of the clergy, for instance. What religious purpose does it serve to dress the part of a bishop, rabbi, or imam? Does the wearer claim a closer relation to God than those who do not wear the symbols of faith? Perhaps there is some hierarchical order imposed by the use of such accoutrements, as in the military, but I suggest that to equate faith with looking the part would be a mistake.

In the Jewish faith, many worshippers rise momentarily on their toes when they say the word *Adonai* or *God* to be closer to God. Muslims prostrate themselves five times a day at daily prayers. Christians kneel and genuflect in church. Perhaps this makes the worshipper a more observant whatever he or she is. And if they are, are they then more devout? Perhaps they become better people.

What is the purpose of these traditional rituals? Perhaps the group performance of such rituals binds the faithful together with their brethren in a more cohesive and therefore safe and productive community. Perhaps not. The Asian religions have similar rituals, and the primitive religions found in the aboriginal societies and those in Africa are also marked by like displays.

The organization of religion was needed in ancient times to offer an explanation of the physical world because so little facts were then known. When the sun came up and set every day and humans had not yet figured out the world was round, it became central in ancient societies that the sun must be the god. It provided light and warmth. It kept predatory animals away from the tribe. It dried the rains and helped crops grow as they turned their leaves toward the warmth.

Where did they get the idea that the sun wanted blood sacrifice? The human emotions, conditions, and most of the momentous events that human were to establish had gods that looked favorably or unfavorably on the population and society. So it was inevitable that the population had faith in and gave homage to these powerful gods that played such a large part in their lives.

As time progressed and societies evolved, the forces of nature had less effect on society. Houses were sturdier, and a rainstorm was no longer a calamitous event. Trades became specialized, and hunters and farmers supplied food to plumbers and carpenters. Societies knew more.

Recently children have been going to school and learning any number of subjects. Faith in God, some modern men think, is unneeded and unnecessary. There is, on the face of this opinion, a case to be made. But what do we really know? Remember 90 percent of the sum total of what we know was discovered, uncovered, or developed in just the last few hundred years. So humans have used God for comfort, order, morality, binding the community together for protection, and survival for these last couple of thousand years, and because we have discovered the elemental parts of mass and matter, we have determined that God is no longer useful, needed, or even exists in this year 2018.

Western European society knows enough about the mysteries of the world—physical, spiritual, emotional, and in all ways things are measured and categorized—to reject faith and turn churches into dance halls, restaurants, and hotels. In a secular progressive society, there can be no room for God or faith. It is in direct competition with the state, which secular progressives seemingly worship. It must be destroyed because it is bad, they say. It seems that it is really hard to defend faith these days, and I posit that organized religion is at least half the reason. We could fill this book with examples of that.

Look no further than the disgraceful behavior of pedophile priests (and other faith's clergy to a degree, to be fair).

"Gee, Mrs. O'Malley, so sorry your son was sodomized after serving mass. The guilty party will be banished to another parish. That will change his future behavior. We will pray for him and your son."

It's a much harder sell to get Mrs. O'Malley to put her weekly offering in the collection plate, to be sure. In fact, many faced with that situation stop coming to church. Some miss the faith of their upbringing; others don't.

Or when the pope comes out and takes a side on a political issue like global warming, here is a bitterly contested proposition. Half the population is convinced this is settled science. And it may well be. The other half, challenging the validity of the science, is sure it's a hoax. And it may well be. The battle rages so strongly that families stop talking. Friendships are lost. Is this a place for the pope to pick a side? Alienating the half that feels otherwise?

The words in the Quran have been translated to English many times. Perhaps losing something in the translation or possibly not. Do they not impose a strict code of behavior on women in particular? Do they not allow believers to treat their enemies as less than human, and are not nonbelievers given the choice of conversion or death? Is not Sharia law the civic observance of the Holy Book's teachings? The most observed religion in the world is also, in Western civilization, the most feared.

Having been raised in a society that was founded on Judeo-Christian principles, most of us are immersed in the society, the culture, and the thought processes. I might suggest that most of the population of these United States have never given that fact a second thought. They have simply accepted it. Most are so deep in the swamp and up to their ass in alligators that it is impossible to remember or see what they are doing in the swamp in the first place.

It goes back to the Ten Commandments, the tablets that God gave to Moses on Mount Sinai. Some years ago, a wise man or woman said that everything you need to know in life, your mother taught you before your fourth birthday. Who could disagree? Similarly, the Ten Commandments lay out a moral code that allows our society to function, avoiding anarchy, bestowing order, and thus allowing progress. Without some moral code and the rules and laws that follow, there is only anarchy. So for hundreds of years, these United States have prospered under an idea that everyone has rights and everyone needs to be valued and respected, along with their rights. Good behavior is desirable; bad behavior is undesirable. These are the simple things that have raised the bar on what a society can accomplish for and with its people, if simple rules, based on simple truths, are used to guide the progression of the society's development through time.

And speaking of these God-given rights or natural rights, as they are often referred to, what are they, and what do they do for us? There is life, liberty, and the pursuit of happiness. Does it seem reasonable?

The next time someone whom you know thinks they have little room for God in their life talks about their rights, ask them this. If they are your rights that you are given at birth, from where and from whom do these rights flow? And what makes them a right? Bestowed upon you from where by whom? Usually the answer is silence with a pained facial expression. Some people do not like the truth pointed out to them.

What about the right of free health care? A democratic socialist on the television news was proclaiming that it's a natural right. Was he wrong? Right or wrong, where did that idea come from? And where might it be going? And the pragmatic among us will waste no time asking who is going to pay for it. The indisputable natural rights of life, liberty, and the pursuit of happiness beg the same question: Who is going to pay to produce, nurture, and ensure that conditions are met to allow those natural rights to take hold, prosper, and be protected?

These things are complicated. And although there has been much discussion these last several hundred years about this topic, there is no definitive consensus yet reached. It sounds like it's every man or woman for himself or herself. Clearly, many of these conditions can only be reached by a concerted effort of the society. But what we know about this organization of people, societies, and governments still leaves much to be desired. We may look at the pinnacle of these achievements as the Constitution of the United States with its three coequal branches of government and separation of powers. But remember this: the founders knew that this effort in self-government was an experiment. In the eighteenth century, it had never really been tried before. There were serious doubts that it would succeed.

Today in the midst of a cold civil war of ideologies in America, we are guaranteed nothing. We can be optimistic for the republic, but we must continue to be vigilant and to participate. We all have voices that must be heard in a constructive civil discourse. If we stop talking, teaching, listening, and arguing, we are done. Being in the midst of this experiment in self-government, it becomes clear that there is a lot about it that we don't really know. It's difficult to understand where the proper perspective is to view it from.

As the rock we ride through space hurtles through time and

whatever else we do not understand toward an unknowable future in every sense of the word *unknowable*, we would rather argue about whose ancestors occupied an arid piece of land first because that will make a difference about who occupies it now. Doesn't that seem like a petty position to take? Small potatoes?

We seem to know little to nothing about everything, and yet the only thing we seem to value is our collective ego and the few nuggets of knowledge that we know little about and cling tightly to but are sure we know everything about. Is that not the same position the Incas and Mayans were in when they were offering blood sacrifices to the gods so the sun would continue to rise or the crops would be fertile? Don't forget that the time of these ancients was only a few thousand years ago. It's just a microscopic scratch mark on the timeline of history. If that doesn't make a reader feel small, understand this: we are very, very small.

I'll paraphrase something I recently heard somewhere in the electronic media but cannot attribute. If you were not born in these United States somewhere in the last 250 years, your only choices in life were peasant, slave, subject, or serf. Hmm. Does that not prove to the reader that self-government a good thing? Consider that half the world's countries still have monarchies. Monarchies! Can you imagine? The ruler of a society is made its ruler because of whom his parents were. Is there a more arbitrary or capricious piece of nonsense on the planet? No doubt this is exactly why in only 250 short years the United States has sprung to world dominance, far outpacing the societies with monarchies!

And I will propose something seemingly twice as absurd as that: democratic socialists want to bring that back! Not in the form of kings and queens but in the formation of a similar structure they will not call the ruling class but will certainly be the ruling class. Their opponents may call it the "deep state." I believe that their project is already underway.

Many of the things that our fathers, grandfathers, and great-grandfathers fought and often died for on foreign soil over the last century seem to be under assault, albeit not very persuasively in my view. In fact, features of this argument, like freedom of speech, are now routinely cherry-picked and used against the forces that produced, fought for, and protected the same right. For example, antifa may point to their right to speak their opinions against the armed forces, the very armed forces that protect their right to speak. However, others are not allowed, by way of being shouted down by similar organizations, from expressing often contrary opinions.

In the service of moving large amounts of world trade and cargo on merchant vessels, this is globally known in that industry as the principle of "Hooray for me and fuck you." Crude? Of course. Accurate? Doubtless.

Another example of the timeless principle of "hooray for me and fuck you" is a story mined from a lighter vein, once told by another very old, very addled senior merchant sea captain. Upon its conclusion, we will then be moving forward. But the telling is far too entertaining and enlightening to pass up.

There once was a small coastal tanker, the name long forgotten, but the captain was in the years preceding WWII a young and single chief officer on this small but sturdy time-worn steel vessel. The route the vessel plied and its sole responsibility was to refuel Arctic ice stations in the far north of Greenland and other far-flung frozen hellholes, areas populated only by reindeer, lichen, and misanthropes. After weeks and weeks up in the ice, risking frostbite and drowning on each and every watch stood, the small vessel would pull into Thule, Greenland, to take on provisions, its own fuel, and fuel for the ice stations. Crew scheduled to go home would leave from Thule, and fresh crew members would join.

So the vessel pulled into Thule. Our chief mate was really looking forward to going ashore and doing all the things that non–chief mate male humans need to do, crazy things like buy a magazine, have a beer or two, pick up some new socks at the small store in town, find a newspaper, sit in a barber's chair, perhaps say hello to and maybe even flirt with a woman, and sit on a bench and watch people walk by—all the things you don't get to do when you are spending weeks and months refueling ice stations in the Arctic in the winter in the ever-present dark, endeavoring to neither freeze nor drown.

Since the captain and the chief mate are generally not allowed to be off the vessel at the same time for safety reasons, the captain agreed to stay aboard while the mate went ashore in his reasonable quest to perhaps feel human again, if only for a short while.

The vessel was alongside its berth. The crew was finishing tying up the ship, and the chief mate was supervising, feeling excited that he was finally going to get to go ashore for a couple of hours and slowly regain a little sanity.

Suddenly, the watertight steel door burst open on the back of the forward house. Out popped the captain, an old Swede who cut his teeth on sailing ships. He approached the chief mate and said in his thick Swedish accent, "Mr. Mate, you stay on board for a few hours. I'm going ashore for a short time, and I'll be back so you can get ashore."

Trouble, no doubt, the chief mate thought. He just nodded and tried not to look as steamed as he suddenly had become.

So all through the night, the next day and night, and the one after that, the chief mate pounded the deck, storing and provisioning the vessel, discharging ballast water, reloading with fuel for the ice stations, swinging repair parts aboard on the cargo boom amidship, taking dry stores, and discharging and signing on the crew, normally the captain's job. But the captain was nowhere to be found.

Three days after arrival, the ship was fully provisioned, stored, and fueled. It was laden to the Plimsoll mark, crewed fully. And all repairs were complete. The vessel was ready to sail. Ahead were another several months in the ice, well north of the Arctic Circle, with eternal nights, dangerous ice, and continuous poor visibility and rough seas. Still there was no captain.

Finally, there came a cab down the dock. It pulled up in front of the gangway on the ship. The door flew open, and a howling banshee of negative energy burst out and fell facedown on the frozen macadam. Splat!

Yelling unintelligible curses at the driver and slamming the door so hard the entire cab shook, the captain wheeled around wildly, and up the gangway he staggered. A miasmic cloud of bad breath and alcohol enveloped him. The chief mate just stood at the top of the gangway, silent and glaring.

The captain's suit coat was ripped, his tie was spotted, and the knot had been pulled so tight it would never come off. There was a hole in his left pant's knee, and his shirt was half flapping in the fresh Greenland sea breeze. His split lip was crusted over, his right eye was blackened, and there was a scabbed-over bruise the size of a silver dollar on his cheek. He had obviously not shaved or bathed since he left the vessel, and his hair was greasy, matted, and obviously uncombed.

As he lurched by the mate, making all possible speed toward his cabin, he was heard to remark, "Come on, Mr. Mate. Let's get her the hell out of here and out to sea right now. I hate this fucking place!"

Hooray for me and fuck you! It happens in all fields of human endeavor.

CHAPTER 14

The Point of it all

So we have talked at length about the distinct possibility that there is much we do not know and much to be learned. Granting me that should not be a chore. In every field where there is miraculous and demonstrated excellence, there is still much that we do not know. How much do we not know? That's a difficult question. After all, we have decided previously that you cannot know what you do not know. However, we can offer with great certainty that there is a boatload of things we do not know. So when the agnostics and the atheists positively tell you there is no God, how do they know that's a truth, and how do believers know that is untrue? Where is the evidence?

I try not to get into discussions about the different religions. So often the religious are zealous and contentious. They are ready to fight. I don't want to fight over religion. I find it repetitive and pointless. Besides, the world is already full of fighting religious zealots. They don't need me. I also don't know enough factually about the religions to wield the principles and tenets like a sword, waylaying my enemies with quoted scripture as some do and do well. I will tend to lose factual arguments about them, and that is never any fun.

I'm not sure it's worth finding out what I don't know about the constructs we know as organized religion. We also know where religious fervor often takes us. History, both ancient and recent, is strewn with examples, most always horrifying. It's always overdone, and the outcome is seldom good. If I gave you one example, I could cite another thousand.

But in discussions about God, I'm all in. God seems to me to be another story altogether. I feel like organized religion is humankind's failed and dangerous attempt to use the almost certain existence (to me) of God for our own often political purposes. Sometimes good things come out of it, like the Ten Commandments. Who can argue that a lot of order, progress, and peace has resulted from those Ten Commandments throughout history?

Other times it's the opposite: the witch trials, the Inquisition, and the Crusades. It's death, misery, and torture. It's humankind's perversion through misinterpretation of godly principles. Do we see some of that today in Islam?

Nonbelievers will point to examples such as the suffering child who dies painfully from starvation or some horrendous malady. They will say there is no God because if there were a God, God would not allow this to happen. What would make them take that position? Are they not assuming that were God to exist, God would be a merciful God? I think that is what they are saying. Why is there that assumption that God is merciful? It may be because that organized religion has said so. And how do they know that, we query? How indeed? There are merciful unexplained acts, and there are merciless unexplained acts. Do we know God, if He/She/It exists, as all-knowing? How do we know that? Again, some depictions of organized religion suggest that God is all-knowing.

The afterlife is a major tenet for the organized religions. On the face of things, it looks like a thinly veiled attempt to control the living while they are living. Brilliant ruse, yes? Heaven, hell, carrot, stick, seventy-six virgins, and eternal damnation—really, what's the point? Nothing we could say at this point on the subject hasn't already been said. My head might explode if I were to continue.

The fact is this: There is either an afterlife or there isn't. There either is reincarnation or there isn't. We are far, far away from knowing that, but in adhering to the principles of noknowlogy, I cannot take a side. I think there may be a distinct possibility, bordering on probability, but I will continue to sit this one out and hedge my bets through my personal behavior- just in case.

It seems that many of the counterarguments to the existence of God are not really what they seem. It looks like they are attacks or rebuttals to the tenets of organized religion, not necessarily to the existence of God. Organized religion and the blind acceptance of its dogma by people over the course of time seem to have done more damage to the belief in God than they have to win hearts, minds, and ultimately converts to the belief in God. Perhaps this is why, as previously noted, churches all over Western Europe and North America are being repurposed as condominiums and nightclubs.

Our understanding of this dismal outlook on the furtherance of religious thought and life into the future is missing an important point. That point is that, even when the traditions, teachings, and dogma of any other well-known religions fail us—that is, do not serve as comfort, wisdom, strength, or moral belief, even though this may be true for individuals and groups of people—that does not disprove the existence of God.

Please read the last sentence again slowly because that is *the point.* It's simply using a lens of organized religion to view the myriad of things that we do not know. This is a losing proposition. Of course religion loses, science wins, and secular humanism grows. As we all know more and more, we think we need religion less and less. But this is a fallacy because we have already proven that the more we know, the less we know, and exponentially to boot! Said another way, society is getting exponentially stupider! Don't believe it? Watch television's network news. If your looking for stupid look no further, in process and content.

So instead of looking at the glass that is both half full and half empty at the same time, we must chose to look at it as half full and proceed toward learned wisdom along that line. What you are opposing is no less than the second law of thermodynamics, which states that the universe (and beyond, I posit) is in a constant state of winding down to a place where all higher states of energy will eventually even out with the lower states of energy. This is a brilliant observation, this law, and thus over time the dissipation of energy from any system or object winds down to zero and the system stops, at rest, for eternity. There are more parables than can be written, although many a physicist, philosopher, scientist, mathematician, and thinkers of many stripes have written innumerable tomes on this subject.

Let me propose that I would think there must be a God when

- we allow our minds to travel to the furthest outer reaches of space and then beyond that;
- we watch the sun set over the horizon;
- we watch a butterfly hatch;
- a painter paints a painting so powerful that people are moved to tears;
- a poet writes a poem so meaningful in so few, carefully chosen words that the poet is not just an artist with immense talent but a vessel between God and the rest of us;
- you close your eyes and listen to a good string quartet;
- a mother wakes in the dark, early morning with a start and then later receives a call from her adult child, injured in an accident that occurred at the precise time of her waking;
- a feeling of déjà vu is so strong that it sends a shiver down a person's spine;

- truly miraculous things happen for no apparent reason or don't; and
- every time a living being of any worldly species takes its first breath in the miracle of birth.

I am convinced in the existence of a Creator, and more importantly, it takes precious little faith for me to hold that belief constant. In fact, it seems to me to be so patently obvious that it is a stretch to entertain that it could be otherwise.

These are the emotional rationalizations of God's existence. Following are the logical and rational explanations.

Even more compelling to me is this: Consider the mathematical odds of God's existence. In a system where we are talking about infinity—of ideas, knowledge, time, distance, planets and stars, or an infinite realm of possibilities—can the work of Patrick A. P. Moran in statistics and probabilities take us in a full circle to prove almost conclusively that there must be a God. Perhaps?

Shouldn't there be a reasonable chance that in all there is out there circling around those infinite possibilities, there just may be a God? That there should be God?

The reader may fairly argue at this point: "So this is it? Is that all this guy's got? I read the whole damn book, and his best argument is that God exists because there are infinite possibilities? This man is an idiot, a charlatan, a snake oil salesman, or all three!"

I would then resort to this retort. If a tree falls in the forest and there is no one there to hear it, does it make a sound? Probably, bordering on "of course it does." But can you prove it makes a sound? No. Nobody who's not there has ever heard a tree fall in a forest that they are not in. But your common sense, faith, and intuition tells you that it makes a sound.

Better yet, let's assign numerical odds to the proposition that a tree makes a sound when it falls in the forest. Let us say a gazillion-to-one for making a sound. Actually, let's up the ante to a hundred gazillion-to-one. I could and would safely bet my life on that proposition, and so could you. Correct?

There, the fact that you, just a moment ago, took the odds, however safe, means that you have faith. You have a belief in something not provable. Isn't that the definition of faith? Congratulations! You are a man or woman of faith! How much faith in this particular case? Not much faith is required, we'll agree, but faith nonetheless

Now, let's go to the furthest opposite end of the faith spectrum, 180 degrees and many light-years away from the last example. Answer this question carefully: How much faith would you have, being the man or woman of faith that we have just demonstrated that you are, that Jesus rose from the dead after crucifixion in Jerusalem over two thousand years ago?

Suppose for a moment you answer, "No way! I'm an atheist, and there's no way that anybody, even Jesus, rose from the dead."

Personally, I wouldn't put it exactly in those terms, but my skepticism basically gets the nod over my faith on this singular and specific example with yours. Of course it does. I was raised a Jew. But in all fairness, I don't actually know that. Do I? Have you ever seen the shroud of Turin? My faith is such that there is a possibility in my mind that it might have happened. A billion Christian people on earth believe that it happened.

When I walked on the Via Dolorosa in Jerusalem and placed my hand on the station of the cross where Jesus fell while carrying that cross, something made the hair stand up on the back of my neck! But that's not proof of anything. I'll willingly agree that by themselves those anecdotes proves nothing. But what about the ten million people whose unshakable faith in anthropomorphic climate change means the world will end in twelve years (eleven years and three months actually if you are keeping track). Many have faith, an almost religious faith, in this prospect. It's odd! Might that not make climate change a religion?

Are you still with me? Then think about this: We have explored a fraction, a tiny slice, of what we do not know, mere glimpses.

We are still attempting to plumb the depths of noknowlogy and always will be, as long as the species survives. We may yet agree that there are things that we will never know because of the limitations of our intellect, with all due respect to the mutant thinker Albert Einstein, one of the few demonstrable exceptions. The possibilities truly are endless. They can never be counted. It's infinite by definition. How much faith does it take to believe that somewhere in the vast fertile infinity of existence, dimensions, gravity and space, and, even possibly, in a microbe on some flea dirt on an intergalactic dog's south end, there is a power higher than ourselves—the Creator? God? Something or someone, in some dimension somewhere, all of which will continue to be unknown for, pardon this, "God knows how long"?

How much of a reach, a stretch really, is it to believe that this may be even partly, in the smallest of ways, the truth? I propose to you that it takes about as much faith to believe in that as it does to believe a tree makes a sound when it falls in the forest. It's very little, just a smidgeon.

As a point of fact, I put my personal faith in the resurrection of Jesus much higher on the "likely so" scale than the belief that the earth will end in twelve years due to climate change, which I find preposterous, disingenuous, and purposefully and evilly alarmist. Sorry, everybody gets to have and hold an opinion. That's mine, particularly when carbon dioxide is named as the culprit. It's the same chemical that we all know to be plant food, for those who never studied photosynthesis.

If that were to be true, would nonbelievers accept that, or would they continue to deny? So I proffer this: with the odds so greatly in favor of it based on what we do not know, there must be a God. Common sense tells me that. The world I observe daily while fending off alligators tells me that. The mathematics of probabilities joins in to tell me that, my beating heart tells me that, the progress of my children tells me that, and an infinite number of anecdotes tells me that. Observed and verified miracles tell me that.

What's my part? What's my contribution? It's just the smallest, nearly imperceptible, barely detectable movement toward and acceptance of faith in the proposition that God exists. What's my sincerest hope? That this book has opened that possibility for you too. The principle here is too important not to have tried.

Thank you.

TEAR OUT THIS PAGE
TAKE IT WITH YOU TO THE WORLD FAMOUS
GASPAR'S GROTTO TAMPA, FLORIDA
THIS IS YOUR COUPON FOR A FREE SHOT AND A BEER
WITH CAPTAIN SCHILLER AND TANKER RAY THE
BARCAT,
AND, IF LUCKY, A RIBALD SEA STORY, UNFIT TO
PRINT,
BUT RIPE TO BE TOLD.
THOSE UNDER 21 WILL BE KEEL HAULED AND
CEREMONIOUSLY
EJECTED BY THE MASTER AT ARMS, MR. VIPER.